Painting a Time
in text and photographs

THE DIARY OF CAROLINE ATHERTON DUGAN

1873-1878

Factory Village

Painting a Time
in text and photographs
The Diary of Caroline Atherton Dugan

Published by Brewster Ladies' Library
Copyright 2014 Brewster Ladies' Library Association, Brewster, MA
All rights reserved.   Published 2014.   *First Edition.*

ISBN 978-0-9828122-4-2

The publication of this diary was made possible with a grant
from The Mary-Louise Eddy and Ruth N. Eddy Foundation.

The images are from the Caro A. Dugan collection,
courtesy of The Brewster Historical Society.

To purchase a copy of this book, contact:
Brewster Ladies' Library
1822 Main Street, Brewster, MA 02631
508-896-3913 • www.brewsterladieslibrary.org

Book and Cover Design by Nancy Viall Shoemaker of West Barnstable Press

Table of Contents

Acknowledgements

At first glance, the publishing of a diary did not seem to be a complex task. After all, we were not writing the book. And then the lesson began...

Kay Dorn, our editor, transcribed, proofed and indexed the entire manuscript. Her dedication to this project was extraordinary. Not only did Kay work on this project faithfully for the last two years, she had championed the publishing of Caro's diary for many years.

Kathleen Remillard, archivist of the Brewster Ladies' Library, provided extensive research to determine the provenance of the diary and the accuracy of the index. She selected the photographs for the diary and volunteered numerous hours of proofreading. She, too, had championed the publication of Caro's diary for many years.

Nancy Viall Shoemaker, our publisher and book designer, gave us advice and support that kept us on track and motivated. The project was delayed several times. Nancy was always there to keep it on target.

Karen North Wells, Underground Art Gallery, rendered exquisite pen and ink drawings of the flowers Caro described in her diary. Karen dedicates these drawings to the memory of her husband, Malcolm Wells, who had originally agreed to create the illustrations.

Sally Gunning, well known author, contributed the introduction for the diary, setting the stage and enticing the reader into Caro's world.

Teresa Lamperti, archivist of the Brewster Historical Society, assisted us with the selection of photographs for the diary and contributed historical documentation.

The Brewster Historical Society generously gave us permission to use the images from the Caro A. Dugan collection.

Ellen St. Sure, archivist for the Town of Brewster, contributed her extensive knowledge and expertise, along with creative ideas for future projects.

Sue Carr, former Brewster Ladies' Library Director, who along with Kay Dorn and Kathleen Remillard made up the original team championing the publication of this beautiful work.

The Mary-Louise Eddy and Ruth N. Eddy Foundation which provided the funding for this project to preserve a primary document of Brewster history and make it accessible to the public.

Kathy Cockcroft, *Brewster Ladies' Library Director*

Introduction

Caroline Atherton Dugan (Caro) was born March 26, 1853, to James and Helen (Cobb) Dugan, in Brewster, Massachusetts, in the home built by Caro's great grandfather, the renowned shipmaster Elijah Cobb. (This house still sits, looking much as it did 100 years ago, at 739 Lower Road). Caro Dugan trained as a kindergarten teacher, although she did not continue in that field. While at Brewster, she helped organize the Brewster Ladies' Library and served as its librarian. After the death of her mother in 1897 she left Cape Cod for Brookline, spending twenty-five years as governess to the five children of Henry and Margaret Whitney, returning each summer to Cape Cod, where she developed considerable skill as a photographer under the tutelage of Cornelius Chenery, a boarder in the Dugan home. (Oral family history suggested a romantic relationship between the two as well).

After her service to the Whitney family came to an end, Caro returned to the family home on Cape Cod, where she took in paying guests to augment her income. At Caro's death on her eighty-eighth birthday in 1941 she left behind her collection of photographic glass plates (now in the possession of The Brewster Historical Society), a published collection of plays entitled *The King's Jester*, and a diary encompassing the years 1873 to 1878, (now in the possession of Brewster Ladies' Library).

One might read Caro Dugan's brief life story and wonder why we care about her diary, why the dedicated staff and volunteers at Brewster Ladies' Library have put forth such effort to bring it before the reading public. In talking with others familiar with the diary I discovered that each cares about it for different reasons. Some most appreciate Caro's meticulous and at times effusive descriptions of the flora that appeared to occupy a large part of her day and her creative imagination; others are fascinated by the colorfully painted glimpses into Brewster's past; still others are intrigued by the sensitively portrayed human interactions among a cast of characters whose names are familiar, at least in part, to anyone who has ever read a road sign or a gravestone on Cape Cod. "A heavy dew this morning silvered the asparagus bushes, & hung on every leaf and blade of grass," she writes on one day, and on another, hinting a familiarity with William Blake, "Tiger lilies are burning bright under the smoke tree." She records the blowing down of the Unitarian Church steeple in a storm, the building of a fish weir, ice house and fish house at Paine's Creek, of ". . . sad news of two of our absent sea captains. Their ships, both loaded with coal, have been burned at sea, and the human freight tossed about on the stormy ocean for days . . ."

Still later she wrote with touching appreciation on the death of her old neighbor, shipmaster, and longtime Representative to the General Court, Captain Solomon Freeman: "He has been gradually failing for a year, running down like a faithful watch worn out with years of service." But offsetting these somber notes, she takes time to record that "Little Bennie Tubman drank a fabulous number of mugs of lemonade & swallowed a tin whistle on top of that!"

My personal appreciation of Caro Dugan's written record must include all of the above, but perhaps I am most drawn to the self-portrait she paints of a woman ever-curious, ever-seeking, ever-striving and bold, sometimes trapped in the confining woman's world of late nineteenth century Brewster, but sometimes soaring wild and free, pushing against – and at times breaking through -- the conventions of the day. On January 1, 1874, she writes: "It seems to be my lot to spend another winter on Cape Cod, though I long for city life & activities. Well, country life is pleasant, even in the winter, -- indeed the real winter can be known only in the country." Confined on Cape Cod she may have been, but she refused to remain confined indoors, or even in Brewster. She writes of a moonlight row across Cobb's Pond, of running in the fields at sunset, of climbing onto the roof at three a.m. to watch an eclipse of the moon, of "hardly tak[ing] the time to finish dressing, because of the beauty out of doors," a beauty which just happened to be formed by a December frost. In a driving easterly storm she and several friends set out to discover the wilds of the back side: "[We] drove to Nauset in the pelting wind & rain. It is a sandy, desolate place on the outside of the Cape, only one dwelling house & three light house towers. The ocean rolls and thunders at the base of the high sand cliffs, coming in in great rollers a translucent green . . . and beyond the surge we had glimpses only of the gray tossing waste of water."

Throughout Caro's diary her love of the written word is evident. Found reading *Hiawatha* at the age of five, and being told she couldn't possibly understand what she was reading, she acknowledged the truth of the remark but added, "I like the jingle of the words." Later in life she clearly spent a good deal of time learning to make her own words "jingle" -- she writes of the wind in the treetops as a "Beethoven wind," a wind in the chimney as a "Viking of a wind"; she describes a mist "overwhelming meadow, wood, village, and sea, even the constant light houses across the Bay . . ."

A peek at any of Caro Dugan's year-end reading lists will further illustrate her love of the written word but also her interest in the world beyond Cape Cod, and perhaps reveal, as well, some of her frustration at being unable to spread her wings as far as they yearned to go. Among the Dickens, Hugo, Tennyson and Thoreau we find books with titles like *Venetian Life, Italian Journeys, Boys of Other Countries, Pictures of Europe, Letters from Italy* and *Switzerland, American Girl Abroad.* But this too we must especially admire about Caro Dugan's diary – however much she yearned for world adventures that were denied her, she never allowed that yearning to diminish the view closer to home. On a train ride to Boston she thoroughly enjoyed talking with an older gentle-man who told her about "hospitals & Parrott guns, carpet looms, & pin factories, engines & coins and precious stones," and once in town reveled in the theater and musical performances and social evenings, but on her trip home she was reminded, as so many of us are, how delightful it is to return to this unique bit of sand. "My sea, and the white gleam of the cliffs over the water, and the deli-cious breeze so salt and strong! How I love it all!" How glad we are that she did, and that she left behind this delightful, jingling record to remind us just why it is that we love it, too.

Sally Gunning

Editor's Notes

The provenance of Caroline Atherton Dugan's diary was discovered in the 1941 recorded minutes of the Brewster Ladies' Library Association. The minutes show that on October 1, 1941, the secretary of the Brewster Ladies' Library was instructed "to write to Mrs. Frank B. Duveneck thanking her for the gifts of Miss Dugan's books and letters." Caro had served as a governess to Josephine Whitney Duveneck. Miss Dugan's former charge, wrote in her autobiography, that "Miss Dugan" was with the Whitney family for twenty-five years, excluding two months each summer when she returned to Cape Cod. After Caro died on March 26, 1941, her books and letters were sent to the Brewster Ladies' Library.

Caro entered her diary in two separate notebooks – one, which we call Volume I, with its marbled cover, is eight by ten inches. It contains no lines, but is written in perfect symmetry. The second, Volume II, is five by seven inches, with a solid grey cover. It appears originally to have contained lines, but they since have faded.

Caro began her daily entries when she was 20 years old. Volume I covers her life during the years 1873 through 1876; while the second book reveals her activities in 1877 and 1878.

There are pages cut from her original entries – we can only speculate they included activities she did not want others who may read it in the future to see them. We have not altered the transcription other than inserting brackets [ ] when her format does not agree with current standards, while parentheses ( ) in the text are Caro's own.

It is appropriate that these memoirs are being published by the Brewster Ladies' Library because Caro was active for many years helping to develop this treasure. She was elected librarian on January 8, 1876 and served until 1879. Later Caro was on the Library Board of Directors from 1917 -1928. Volume II of the diary was written while Caro was the librarian and will appeal to those who are curious about the library. Her words will also be of interest to those who enjoy Brewster history or who marvel at the social changes in the daily lives of young women in the 1800s, compared to now. Also of interest will be Caro's daily reporting of which flowers, trees and shrubs are peeking out in bloom that day.

The idea of presenting Library history started in 2002, when Sue Carr, then Library Director, decided to publish the diary of Sarah Augusta Mayo, the founder of the Brewster Ladies' Library. The book, *Looking Back*, is available at the Library. Following this publication, Sue directed the transcribing of the beginning of the BLL Board of Directors' minutes. These are in two volumes – *The First One Hundred Years*, and *The Next Fifty*, and are housed in the Cape Cod section of the library. The history project lay dormant for several years until our present Library Director Kathy Cockcroft applied for and received a grant from the Mary-Louise Eddy and Ruth N. Eddy Foundation to publish the diaries.

Kay Dorn, *Editor*

VOLUME I

December 26, 1873 through December 26, 1876

1873

December 26. Friday.

George & Theo went in early train. Theo starts on his business life, now. I read to Frank in "Little Dorrit."

December 27. Saturday.

Frank went in noon train.

December 29. Monday.

Emily went in noon train. I went to tea at Nettie's.

December 30. Tuesday.

Alice Crosby called at twilight.

December 31. Wednesday.

The year is ended. Twelve rings out from the old clock in Middle room. The year brought many pleasant things: the three weeks housekeeping with aunt Mame and our Shakspeare** readings; the perfect "diamond day" of ice jewelled trees & earth – a wonderful sight; new books; lovely walks and rides; the hours spent with dear Relief* Freda's visit; Winnie boy's homecoming; three weeks among the Vermont hills; our pleasant Thanksgiving.

Relief Paine was a Brewster resident, blinded and partially paralyzed from a fall down stairs when she was 16. She inspired daily visitors who loved and admired her. For more, see Anna Howard Shaw; The Story of a Pioneer; Chapter 6, "Cape Cod Memories."

** *Throughout this diary, with two exceptions (Dec. 19, 1878, and Books Read in 1878 list) Caro spells Shakespeare without the first e.*

Left: Nettie's west avenue leading to the Allen-Cobb house (Roland Freeman) - torn down; was next to country store.

1874

January 1. Thursday.

It seems to be my lot to spend another winter on Cape Cod, though I long for city life & activities. Well, country life is pleasant, even in the winter, – indeed the real winter can be known only in the country. It is not here yet, however. What strange weather we are having! More like spring than winter, these mild misty days.

January 2. Friday.

Another gray, wet day, the rain drip, dripping from the eaves. Toward evening a faint rosy light began to show through the gray. It deepened & spread, until the west was all aglow with color.

January 4. Sunday.

I love my outlook. As I write, I glance out on the little grass-grown garden under my window, and my eyes linger with a pleased fondness on the low hedge of arbor vitae that shuts it in; the grassplot in whose centre is a mossy, cracked stone vase which is empty now, but in summer is running over with green vines; the narrow flower beds that edge it; the sentinel fir in one corner, so tall & straight & slender. Beyond the garden I see the road bordered by silver abeles, & curving westward; and beyond the road are wide brown fields in one of which a pretty pool of water lies under a great willow. In the distance gleam white village houses, and a wooded swamp shuts out the view of Scargo hill, – Our west parlor is full of sunshine. Mother sits at a south window where she can look out on the front yard with its great trees – ailanthus and silver poplars, two on either side, their arching boughs nearly meeting overhead, and my hawthorn bush, bare and brown today, but in spring all one flush of pink blossoms, and up the winding lane.

January 8. Thursday.

A walk at sunset, facing a glorious west wind, so fresh and cold after the late enervating breezes. The heavy curtain of cloud has at last rolled away and I gaze into depths of wonderful sky, most purely, delicately blue. Great banks of snowy cloud in the east and the west a wide reach of clear, pale yellow light that was almost white and gave a misty, unreal look to the Dennis hills, the winding road, and quiet pools of water in the fields.

Elijah Cobb House 1889

January 9. Friday.

At last! I opened my eyes this morning to see bright rays dancing about my chamber. Springing to the window, I opened it <u>wide</u> to let in the glorious sunshine & pure, fresh air. Oh, the delicious cold – like a draught of iced nectar! The strong west wind set the blood fairly dancing in my veins. The little snowbirds were singing, & the bright waters leaping & sparkling in the sunlight. It was like a resurrection. This afternoon I walked to Relief's, coming back in the quiet evening. The wind had dropped, the sun had set, but the west was bright with after glow and in the deepening blue overhead the stars shone out. The tall rushes by the roadside stood motionless, & the quiet hush was broken only by the faint twitter of birds now & then.

When walking down, I was overtaken by an old woman, who, after learning that I was Elijah Cobb's granddaughter, told me of her life and sorrows. She had moved from Brewster to Harwich ten years ago, and her name was Burgess. Her husband, three sons and three nephews had enlisted in the war of the Rebellion, and not one had lived to come back. She had one daughter left who married a sailmaker, and two months ago, while at work, some splints of wood flew into his eye, resulting in total blindness. Her husband died in Libby prison of starvation and scurvy, and also a nephew. One of their comrades lived to come home and tell the tale. "Joshua" (her husband) she said, "had

3

a fine set of teeth, white & strong. I've seen him with my own eyes bite a board nail in two, but before he died, his teeth could be bent in any direction. He never shaved after entering the prison, and with his long beard and wasted face, he must ha' looked frightful ghastful." She told me with evident pride that her sons were all under age and could not be drafted, but they were eager to go. Albert, the eldest and apparently the favorite, was but nineteen, and the youngest went as drummer boy.

She could not speak of Albert without tears. "He was a noble boy, tall & handsome, with great black eyes. I cannot bear to look at his picture now. He rose to be an officer and after two years service, came home on a furlough. When the time came for him to go again, I clung to him & said "Albert, I can't, oh, I can't let you go back!" –but he held my hands & looked right into my eyes with his black ones, and said "Mother, two things I can never forget – God and my country," – and with that, he went away. I never saw or heard from him again. It is supposed he was shot while on picket duty. He may have died in prison."

Her second son died in a hospital and she went on to Washington to nurse him. She told me much about hospital life, our wounded soldiers and the soldiers graves at Washington.

"They tell me I should be proud to have given so much to my country. It may be wicked, but I can hardly feel so yet. If only one had come back, but to lose all! Ten years ago, but I am not reconciled yet. If they had all been shot in battle, – but to starve to death! Oh, those prisons!"

Within a short time, she had lost the use of one hand, and now had come back to her native town to see if she could recover a pension of her eldest son's that she had not yet received. She did not forget the sorrows of others in her own great grief, for she told me of a poor boy dying of consumption in the eastern part of the town, whom she had visited this afternoon. "Leife [sic] has not happiness for me any more," she said, "I am only looking forward to being called away; but there is still good to be done in the world. Life is meant for that, is it not?" Then, with a regretful glance at her disabled hand, – "My working time is past now. I can do but little to help others, but kind words and wishes are better than nothing." She must have been very pretty in her youth, and still the poor thin face under the gray hair attracted by its blue eyes and tearful, patient smile. She was uneducated, but her patient spirit made the plain language both eloquent & pathetic.

January 14. Wednesday.

A driving snowstorm. The roads drifted high, & the snow falling fast. Toward evening, the sun came out for a short time, and I went out with Steenie and May, helped build a fort and snow man, and we had a merry snow ball frolic. Little May was a picture in her blue and white wrappings with glowing cheeks and shining curls powdered with snow.

January 23. Friday.

A wild night. Heavy black masses of cloud sweeping across the sky; the moon, when not totally obscured, giving a pale dim light; the trees throwing black gigantic shadows on the ground; the wind moaning in their branches.

January 30. Friday.

A stinging cold day. Isaac Freeman came with Jerry to take me to Relief's. The drive was much like flying, the light tilbury bounding over the frozen roads, for Jerry went at lightning speed apparently as much excited as myself by the intense cold.

February 2. Monday.

I have been reading Whipple on "Wit and Humor." I must read something of Rabelais, Dean Swift & Sydney Smith, especially Swift's pamphlet giving a statement of reasons for its being on the whole, impolitic to abolish the Christian religion in England. This is said by Mackintosh to be the finest piece of irony in the English language.

February 6. Friday.

Melissa Crocker (the 'warf, May calls her) was here to sew for us yesterday, and spent the night. Poor little woman! it is touching to see her so brisk and cheery and helpful, in spite of her short, thick, mis-shapen figure (she is hardly taller than May) and poor deformed back. She said today that she sometimes thought hers a pretty heavy cross to bear, but when she thought of Relief's, hers seemed as nothing in comparison. My mother is very good to little Melissa. Snow, rain, wind today, the roads cased in ice, dazzling to the sight, but unsafe for travel.

February 7. Saturday.

Soft & light, through the still air, falls the snow, powdering the dark evergreens, hanging its pearls on every tree & shrub. The little west garden is most lovely, – the arbor vitae hedge hung with delicate snow wreaths, the old cherry tree white with this winter bloom, the grape vine hanging in curves & festoons about the little arbor, the old stone vases over flowing with foamy whiteness.

February 12. Thursday.

Out for a walk today, the first time in two weeks. It is next to impossible to wade through deep drifts or the mixture of snow, ice & mud that blocks our lane through half the winter. Today, the walking was fairly good, though not easy, the sky an unclouded blue and the sunshine warm and golden. I had little May for a companion and was much entertained. She evidently thought that, as I had invited her to walk with me, she must take pains to make herself agreeable. She was greatly delighted with a high snow bank which had curled over at the top and hung down the side like a curtain, shutting in the whitest, daintiest little snow couch imaginable.

February 14. Saturday.

St. Valentine's day, & fresh & lovely after a day of rain. The snow has almost disappeared, and miniature lakes & rivers abound. I crossed the brown, wet fields to the shore this afternoon. Each little hollow was filled with water, blue & clear as the sea itself, and the many beds of moss delicate gray & vivid green seemed to rejoice in the welcome moisture and warm sunshine. Yesterday the bay was full of snow & ice; today hardly a vestige remains. The tide was out, and at least a dozen distinct groups of clam diggers were on the flats, in rough clothing and high fisherman's boots, with hoes and buckets and carts. The strong, salt breeze was invigorating and it was pleasant to watch the gulls – wild, graceful creatures! – skimming over the deep blue channels and brown sands, their wings glancing like silver in the sunlight. Now one of the diggers comes toiling up the cliff, with a heavy bucket of clams slung over his shoulder, and I have his company for a short distance. We had a fine sunset, the whole sky flushed with rosy color, and in the west broad horizontal bars of purple, gold, & crimson, above which floated a great cloud of magnificent rose-gold.

6

February 16. Monday.

Walked to the peat swamp, meaning to enter it in search of mosses, but hastily abandoned my purpose on meeting with a skunk! There was a mutual retreat in opposite directions.

What play days I have known in and about this old swamp! I remember the mighty forest through which Win & I crept with bated breath, expecting encounters with robbers & wild beasts, yet pausing to admire the arches of interlaced boughs above our heads; it is now a dense thicket of underbrush through which I cannot force my way. The water that of old was to us Lake Champlain, the Mississippi river, the Pacific ocean, shrinks to a sluggish black pool. The wonderful islands that dotted its surface, are but bits of rock & old stumps out of which grow mosses & tiny bushes. The long peat house in the field, under whose roof the swallows built their nests, is old and out of repair, but it has been by turns a palace, a fortress, a prison, a robber's cave. The birds still fly in and out, but the happy fancies of childhood flit about it no longer.

The great sand hollow near the pond has served as a bandit's retreat, a canyon, a witch's cave, an Indian or gypsy encampment, and Rome with its seven hills. The old garden has been put to various uses; its grass plot was rolling prairie, – its ditch a canal, a Venetian water way, the river Nile, – its flowers & fruit trees and arbors, the land of enchantment. The little flower garden, shut in by its arbor vitae hedge, has been a castle moat, an old English pleasaunce, fairy land, and Mt. Olympus. What good times we children did have!

February 20. Friday.

Our usual rainy day caller – Capt. Solomon Freeman – has been in, and entertained us with interesting sailor yarns. He told of meeting Washington Irving at Cadiz in 1828. Irving was then at work on his "History of Columbus," and was also sending off at intervals, the M.S. sheets of the "Conquest of Granada." Capt. Freeman dined at the house of a friend, in company with the author, and afterward Irving breakfasted with him on board his ship, and while the ship lay at anchor in Cadiz harbor, they often took long walks together. The captain describes Irving as being the pleasantest & most agreeable companion he ever fell in with, showing a ready adaptability to all places and associates. Capt. Freeman, also, met Cooper the famous novelist, in Marseilles.

It cleared later, and Steenie and I went for a walk in the fields. Hosts of red & brown & gray & green mosses held up their fairy-like cups, and there were beds of thick soft leaves of microscopic size, and moss gardens out of which grew tiny forests of shining red grass tipped with white. Is it not wonderful that each rough fence, or rock or broken bit of board, if left to itself, is quickly seized upon by the soft busy moss fingers & rounded & smoothed & wrapped about until the unsightly roughness is quite hidden under soft grays & browns and greens? I love these darlings of field and wood and wayside, trying in their humble way, to make the world beautiful.

We entered the pine grove. A slender sapling which had taken a sudden bend and turn a few feet from the ground, and then shot straight upward, furnished a natural seat, and I lingered there to enjoy the thick soft carpet of pine needles, the straight, slender living columns, the murmur of the swaying boughs, the golden light that streamed through green vistas from the stained windows of sunset.

Tonight, as often in August evenings, a white sea of mist drifts slowly around the house, out of which the great branches and tops of trees rise ghost-like; yet overhead, in a clear sky, the moon and stars are shining.

February 23. Monday.

Mist & rain. Later, the rain ceased & a strong west wind sprang up, so Steenie and I sallied out to hunt for mosses. The peat water was steel color today, with dark shadows rushing over it at each fresh gust of wind. The wind was playing grandly in the pines today, the grove, like a great harp, giving out solemn music under the touch of his viewless fingers.

One sees such pretty sights in looking for mosses. The holes where fence posts have been uprooted, are converted into elfin chambers, roofless, but hung with rich green tapestry of the finest texture, and carpeted with velvet. I lie flat on the ground to gaze & admire.

February 26. Thursday.

Charlie Hall's wedding day. Yesterday was a driving snowstorm, and today men have been at work digging out the roads. One walks up our lane between high walls of snow that shut out all but the blue sky above. Yet at sunset, the blue height of Scargo had the misty look of Indian summer against a golden sky.

March 1. Sunday.

Theo is at home for a week before leaving for the West, to be in Frank Greenleaf's employ at Minneapolis. My lord has grown into a tall, broad chested fellow. Nine weeks absence from home has enhanced its value, and he has taken to lecturing Steenie on his duty to his mother!

March 3. Tuesday.

Rode part way to Relief's, then the road became impassable, and I took to the fields, wading through snow and mud and water to avoid a ditch, and getting tangled in briars. The sea view from the hill top paid for any amount of scrambling. Today, the sun was veiled with thin clouds, and the sea was a changing gray-blue in the softened light. – I read bits of Annie's letters to Relief, and played with the pretty baby Helen.

March 4. Wednesday.

A dark, misty morning, but the warmth and fragrance of spring is in the air, and tiny venturesome green blades are pushing up through the brown earth. All day it rained, but we had a lovely sunset – golden mist, golden sky, golden hills.

March 5. Thursday.

Rode down & spent two hours with Relief. The school house pond was a pretty sight, the cool dark blue water dimpled all over with glancing sunbeams, and the white-capped waves in the Bay were having a rough & tumble frolic.

March 7. Saturday.

The air was filled with the hissing of tiny fine flakes of snow, which toward noon changed to rain & then to driving sleet which stung my face as I walked to the Library.

Brewster Ladies' Library

March 9. Monday.

All day, black masses of cloud have brooded over the house, like dark robed angels of Pain & Death. Will brighter days ever come? Poor Abby! hers has been and is a hard life. One's heart aches to see her suffer. If sympathy could but put strength into tired limbs & aching heads! We are <u>so</u> tired with this anxious nursing. Yet through it all, mother is brave & cheerful. Like the crocus, she smiles in the face of snow & rough weather.

March 12. Thursday.

Darker & darker. Outside & in, heavy clouds & oppressive atmosphere. Abby is very ill, delirious half the time. George came last night and was despairing. He did not hear of her illness until yesterday morning, and was told she was very low & he might not find her alive. He watched with her last night, & Emily Lincoln watches tonight. Mother is so tired, it worries me.

March 13. Friday.

Cold, freezing, but clear & bright. The evergreen hedge shines like polished steel in the sunlight, & the mossy trunks of the abeles have apparently turned to solid gold. I long to get out of doors again. The pretty mosses gathered more than two weeks ago are as fresh as ever and retain the faint pleasing odors of wood & field. The odd, bright grass, blood red in color, has grown an inch. Tiny green leaves & grass blades also are pushing their way up through the soft moss. It is my winter garden. Steenie announced the other day that I looked like a "poetress," when writing at my west window, with books, flowers, and the nature of the country (i.e. my moss-filled dishes) about me! – The poor daffodil buds are chilled and drooping. The crocus shoots in the flower garden, huddle close together for warmth, and bid defiance to the north wind.

March 14. Saturday.

Out for a short walk this afternoon, the first time for a week. The sea is blue & open, but the pond still snowbound, shows like a pearl in its setting of dark pines & russet fields. No sign of life in the willows, but their slender drooping branches made a silver tracery against the deep blue of the sky. This delicate winter beauty of the trees cannot be surpassed by the rich leafiness of summer.

I filled my vase with the glossy myrtle leaves which keep green all winter under the snow.

March 15. Sunday.

Walked to the peat swamp with George & May. Found but little of the green, & the red cup moss, but the fields were over run with mosses of delicate, silver-gray.

March 16. Monday.

This morning the earth was silvered with frost which made the brown fields beautiful, and cooled the sweet morning air. The sea and sky were an exquisite pale blue, the cape cliffs encircling the Bay were misty & purple with the morning shadows. Toward noon I walked to the shore with Steenie & May. The dry grass & mosses were crisp & crackling beneath our feet. The pond was still frozen, & showed white, solid ice in its middle, a beautiful, transparent blue around the edges, while close in shore was a long, narrow lane of blue water dancing & dimpling in the sunlight.

The blue sea water was darker and deeper in color than it was this morning. Near shore, great cakes of ice were rising & falling with the waves, and as they came in contact with each other, or gently grounded on the beach, instead of a grinding & grating noise, they gave out a gentle, whispering sound like the sighing of the wind among pine trees. All along the beach stretched a solid wall (at least 3 feet thick and four or five feet in height) of snow & ice thrown up by the sea. The ledges & (and) summits of the rocks were also piled with blocks of snow, which to the children's fancy, took familiar shapes of houses and animals. We met two boys with guns and a dog, looking for sea gulls. We could see the gulls in the distance skimming the waves, and I was heartily glad they were beyond reach. Steenie addressed one of the lads as Darius Green, and we made little May believe him to be the Darius of flying machine fame. It was rather wicked, but great fun later to see her gazing up at the sky in firm belief that a far off gull was the flying Darius, and when she picked up a wild duck's wing, thinking Darius had lost one of his, we laughed in our sleeves at the deluded innocent. I must tell the child it was only a joke. She was delighted with a caterpillar we found one day rolled up in a tiny soft ball, and thought it must be like Rip Van Winkle, sleeping all winter. Children's thoughts are delightfully amusing at times.

I brought home some poverty grass; its soft pearly gray will go well with my myrtle leaves. I love the sober colors of this time of year – the soft grays & browns.

March 19. Thursday.

A warm, strong wind; sea & sky misty gray. I have often noticed that in the early morning, sky & water are of the same color & it is hard to find the dividing line, but as the day advances, the sea deepens & darkens in color. Last Monday, at daybreak, both sky & sea were a clear serene blue, but later in the day the water, tho' blue, was dark & angry, tossed into foam by a strong wind, & swept over by dark shadows. The same sky arched above it, but its blue was rendered back imperfectly, darkened & shaded by the unrest of the troubled waters.

March 20. Friday.

A clear, warm day. I walked up the street as far as the old Elkanah Bangs place. It looked dreary and forsaken. The wind sighed through the trees, the dry leaves rustled underfoot, and long grass & briers waved over the stones & charred relics of the fire. – I called on Mary Tubman and she showed me over her house, a pretty, cosy place enough, though it might certainly bear to be a little cleaner. Two south windows were filled with plants of which she was evidently proud, & with reason. Such abundant leafage, & a wealth of blossoms – great clusters of scarlet geranium white & red petunias, pink Cambridge Pet, & one fragrant beauty of a rose, while all around the room ran the green German ivy. – Mary has the key to the Pratt house & showed me over it today. As a child, I used to shudder at its frowning exterior & hurry past, peopling it with ghosts & goblins. I found the interior in full accord with those childish fancies. Dark stairways & unexpected doors & dismal holes; quaint wall paper, old furniture & wide window seats. There are four large, square rooms on ground floor. One is a dining room, with dark handsome doors, queer narrow closets, & lovely old china-white with a pattern of tiny red leaves. The adjoining room contains a tent bedstead & several curiously carved and twisted chairs. It is hung with pictures, turned face to the wall, among them an oil painting of the wedding morn of Priscilla the Puritan maiden, showing her on her "snow white steer," with Alden beside her, leading the procession through the Plymouth woods. From the dining room we stepped into a dark little hall, & groped our way down a stair with a rope for baluster, to the basement kitchen, a great, gloomy, low-ceiled room opening on places so black that I hardly dared enter. I stepped into a pantry as the least unpromising, but it led to the worst hole of all, a low long rough place, abounding in yawning archways & recesses; & lighted dimly by a dusty hyphen of a window. Upstairs the chambers corresponded in size & number to the lower rooms. One wallpaper looked like a representation of the carboniferous era – immense leaves sprawling over the walls, with a flaming border of great yellow flowers. George Pratt's room has a rough wooden desk and bookcase

Pratt House

that take up one side of it, the latter filled with works on philosophical & scientific subjects. Outside his door are the attic stairs, & lighting a lantern, we crept up into darkness, & poked about in old chests for the two skeletons George made use of in his studies, but unsuccessfully. So I missed an uncanny experience.

Leaving the house, the hall door shut us out with a heavy crash, and passing down the narrow sloping path bordered with box, we turned to look back at the dark mansion with its four solid chimneys. The front yard is full of mulberry trees, and enclosed by a high hawthorn hedge, from which a ruinous fence is falling away by degrees. East of the house is an orchard of low, spreading apple trees, over run with currant bushes. The back yard is shaded by great trees, but leads to miserable sheds & out buildings with floors, roofs, & chimneys quite unsafe. A dismal place, enough! It was a relief to reach my own home and cheery hearth fire.

March 21. Saturday.

The first crocus! This promises an early spring. Already the lilac buds are unfolding & red buds of the ailanthus begin to swell. The bonny crocus blossom! its delicate petals are my delight, the three outer a rich deep purple, the three inner violet, veined with white, and the slender golden shaft in the centre. The robins are here. I saw a number of red breasts yesterday.

March 22. Sunday.

Rode to Relief's for a short goodby call, carried her the first spring flowers.

March 23. Monday.

To Boston in afternoon train. A cold, windy day. Walter met me at the station & escorted me to 7 Chester Square. I have a cosy little room, tho' at the top of house.

March 24. Tuesday.

Went this evening to a little musical party at Mrs Sanborn's.

March 26. Thursday.

My twenty-first birthday. Win sent me a book "Yesterdays with Authors." I went over to exhibition at Inst. for the Blind with Emily, & Mrs Badger. Dined with aunt Mary.

March 27. Friday.

Spent the day with aunt Dede & Fannie Tyler. Fannie was very entertaining, & went over much of her European experience with me, painting graphic word pictures.

April 1. Wednesday.

A strange sunset effect – a great rosy cloud in the west, broken into the semblance of scores of round bright little heads leaning over the gray sky parapet. Child angels, perhaps!

April 5. Sunday.

Easter Sunday. Aunt Mame, Miss Mulliken, Frank Kilbourne & I visited the old North church on Salem St. formerly the Green Lane of Boston. The chimes rang out as we entered the street, – from the first Boston bells, placed there in 1744. The body of the church is plain, but the steeple, designed by Charles Bulfinch, is a fine piece of architecture. The brick is laid in the style of the eighteenth century, called the English Bond, of which but few specimens now exist in Boston. Over the entrance is a plain tablet

Christ Church

1723

It is the oldest church standing, in Boston. The interior has seen considerable alteration, but is still curiously old-fashioned. The chancel is decorated with a painting of Christ at the Last Supper. Also with four large tablets showing forth the Lord's prayer, the commandments & the Creed, over each of which leans the head & wings of a cherub, while higher up is a painting of the Dove, encircled by child angels. On a high desk in the chancel lies a great brown covered Bible, published in 1717 and presented by George II (as also the communion service) to Christ Church in 1733. It belonged to the Vinegar edition (so called from a mistake in the heading of a chapter – the substitution of the word vinegar for vineyard) of which but three copies are now extant, the other two being in England. It is admirably well preserved, considering the years of constant use, and we enjoyed looking at the quaint print & illustrations. To the right of the chancel, in an arched recess, is the first monument erected to the memory of Washington in this country, – a plain slab & simple bust of marble, with no inscription whatever. This bust was carried in Washington's funeral procession, & in its base is a lock of his hair.

The chandeliers are old & curiously shaped, with wax tapers in their sockets. Surmounting the organ gallery are four angels in gorgeous red, blue and purple draperies, blowing at gilded trumpets. The chancel was bright with Easter flowers. I was disappointed in my hope of seeing the bells, but the belfry is closed until the first of May, given over to dust and myriads of pigeons. The sexton was a pleasant, jovial little man who treated us with great courtesy.

We then visited Copp's Hill Burying-Ground, the Mother tomb, &c. Apparently the oldest stone is that of Grace Berry, bearing the date of 1625, before Boston was a settlement. It is splintered & defaced, having been used as a target by King George's soldiers.

On the way home we went into King's Chapel, a beautiful old church with high square pews, stained windows, & memorial tablets. It was fragrant with the breath of flowers that wreathed chancel and chandeliers and monuments.

April 11. Saturday.

Have been spending this week with Emily, but today came back to Miss Dixie's.

This morning my cousin Helen & I visited the Children's Hospital at the corner of Rutland & Washington Sts. We were shown into a reception room where were two of the Sisters in long gray robes with wide hanging sleeves, white bands & close fitting caps, a cross hanging from the neck. We followed one of these, a tall Sister with a plain, pleasing face, upstairs & through the wards, airy, pleasant rooms occupying the three upper stories. Each ward contained a number of single beds, and but few were empty. Sunshine streamed in through the wide windows, over the plants & running ivy, the scattered playthings on the floor, the white beds and pale faces of the sick children. Some were sitting up busy with the toys on their little wooden trays; some, playing little mother to doll babies; others, singing and talking merrily; while a few lay quietly watching the rest, too ill to stir or speak themselves. One of these last was propped up with pillows, her eyes closed, and breath faintly fluttering between white, parted lips – like a waxen figure. "Disease of the heart", the Sister told us. For the past two years, the poor child has been forced to carry heavy loads of wood, water & coal up two flights of stairs. She has only lately been found & brought to the Hospital, & the doctor says will never be well again. It must seem "evingly" to her, here. The children are very young, ranging, I should judge, from two to twelve years of age. The patients are suffering mostly from scrofula or hip disease. They are constantly being discharged & the vacant places filled by new arrivals. The oldest comers have been there two years. The children are interested & amused by visitors. One pretty boy, with golden curls like those of Theo's babyhood, prattled to me about his toy dog. His name was Charlie Sprowl. Little Lizzie, a child of two years, sang to us at the sister's request, a plaintive ditty, rocking her doll gently the while.

April 12. Sunday.

To Hollis St. Church in A.M. to hear Mr Chaney. It is a quiet old church & restful. The organist, Mr Sharland, was quite active, swinging back & forth, from side to side, in time to the music; his bald head now shining out like a full moon, then dwindling to a crescent, then would come a total eclipse, and when I feared the little man had actually lost his balance, his shining poll would beam upon me in full orbed glory again. – There are several boarders at Miss Dixie's; Gen. Haines & wife, handsome & agreeable, Mr & Mrs Tutlock, Mrs Wood & daughters, Miss Miller, a bright school teacher with an ardent lover, and Mr Stedman who is the jewel of the collection. Very short of stature is he with a deformed or wooden leg (it looks like the former and sounds like the latter), stone deaf, and with an affection of the throat which manifests itself in gurgles and groans and growls. He says there is a constant whirring and rushing and roaring in his head and the noise is so great that he cannot hear; it is like a battery, going off now & then in loud reports like cannon. Nevertheless, his temper is admirably serene, and he bows & smiles affably on us all. His face is really pleasant, with its blue eyes & gray moustache, & we like him, altho' we cannot help laughing at his odd, gruff noises! He is wealthy and a bachelor, and I insist that there is a romance in his life, because of the portrait of a slim & sentimental-looking female in old-fashioned attire which hangs in his room. Of course it may be his mother!

April 14. Tuesday.

Aunt Mame & I started at 9.30 A.M. for Cambridge. Called on Mrs Allen Lizzie Munroe's sister, and she gave us a note of introduction to Mrs James of the Bachelaer house. This house was built in 1700 and is a three story brick building, with spacious grounds abounding in trees & shrubbery, flowers and climbing vines. Mrs James was a stately lady with gray hair brushed back from a high forehead in Martha Washington fashion. She was courteous & entertaining, showing her rooms & curiosities & talking delightfully all the while, and seemed pleased with our interest & admiration.

I was interested in a great shallow dish of very old china the central figure on which was a monster with fiery breath and twisted tail, called (as a Japanese college student had explained) a dream-eater, from his eating people's dreams in the morning. – The library was lined with books & hung with fine paintings, and one piece of furniture, half desk, was devoted to

Napoleon Bonaparte, its shelves filled with books relating to him, while the great drawers held volumes illustrating scenes in the Emperor's life. How Steenie would revel in this! He has such an enthusiastic admiration for this man, that I teasingly call him "Napoleon's friend". We dined with Mrs Allen, and I made the acquaintance of her daughter Molly, a bright girl of seventeen. She told me of the death of Annie Handy's father.

April 15. Wednesday.

Visited the Children's Hospital for an hour or two. Several little girls were dressed & playing about the room, and Maggie, a gentle, patient child whose leg was amputated some weeks ago was sitting up for the first time since last Fall. Jennie Comer, the little sufferer from heart disease, was easier today, her dark eyes open & looking eagerly at the flowers in my hand. I gave her a rosebud, & her face lighted up. "She had never seen the country," she said, "but it must be beautiful, if flowers grew there." She liked to watch the window opposite her bed, for outside, the tree branches waved and birds flew in & out. Charlie was in bed, his hands & cheeks burning with fever, & all my efforts called forth only a look from two grieving blue eyes, & a faint "Please, a drink of water."

I took a walk on the Common this afternoon. Was interested in the pretty deer who regarded with gentle curiosity the brown sparrows hopping & twittering at their feet; the old Elm that has seen so many changes; three little ragged girls picnicking on a stone seat & made perfectly happy by a brown paper parcel & contents; a blind old fiddler with bent, uncovered head & white hair streaming in the wind, & an old man on crutches, watching the boys at ball play, with an amused & interested smile.

April 16. Thursday.

Spent the day at Fannie Tyler's. After dinner, aunt Dede went to a florist's & bought flowers to carry to the Children's Hospital. Charlie was better, dressed & playing about, & I held him in my arms a long time, listening to his baby prattle, the golden head resting on my shoulder, & his deep blue eyes looking gravely up at me from under their long lashes. We scattered our flowers among the children, – roses, pinks, mignonette, heliotrope & smilax, keeping the fairest & most fragrant for Maggie and Jennie, & a dainty nosegay for Mother Louisa. I went in again to the boys ward to kiss Charlie goodbye. Bessie, the nurse, had twined one of his flowers with its green leaves in the soft, loose curl that crowns his sunny head, & the bright posy rivalled his cheeks in color.

April 20. Monday.

A pouring rain. After dinner, went to the Hospital for an hour. The doctor was making his daily round. Maggie was suffering & unable to sit up. She is a sweet child, quiet, shy, patient and unselfish, quite a little mother to the younger children. Jennie Comer was asleep, & looked like a frail, white anemone. Her dark eyes opened in time to smile goodbye. It was really hard to look my last at the pleasant room & its pale little occupants.

My first & last words were for little Charlie, whom I found in bed, his crimson cheek pressed against the bars of his iron bedstead, quietly watching the play of the other children. His little frame was shaken by a hard, croupy cough, and every few minutes, he would murmur sadly "Charlie sick!" I gave him my gold pencil to play with, and he brightened a little, sitting up a few minutes, with his curly head resting against my arm, but even the pencil seemed heavy for the little hands, & the child laid himself wearily down again. He has become very dear to me in this short time, but I fear I shall never see him again in this world. Bessie tells me that his mother is dying today. Next to Charlie Sprowl is Freddy's bed, & a bright, happy baby is he, in spite of the heavy weight chaining down his poor little leg. He has brown eyes, pretty dimples, & a thick mat of bronze-brown hair. I helped him build block houses on his wooden tray, & he fairly bubbled over with glee, his laugh as irresistible as the bright rippling of a brook. Mother Louisa shook hands with me warmly at parting. The gray dress of the Sisters will always be pleasing in my sight since I have known her.

I took tea with Mrs Badger, & went to Boston Theatre with her in evening, to see Miss Leclerq in the "New Magdalen."

April 21. Tuesday.

Aunt Nettie, Emmie & I took the morning train for the Cape. The ride was tiresome, but we revived at the first whiff of salt air, & the sight of sea water, & the curve of white cliffs in the distance.

April 24. Friday.

Steenie brought me mayflowers today in color like tinted sea shells, fresh & fragrant.

April 25. Saturday.

A driving snowstorm!! Winnie came.

April 27. Monday.

Green grass again. A glorious sea, clear, pale green, with great, rushing breakers. Aunt Mame came home.

April 30. Thursday.

Walked to Relief's, fighting my way against a strong north wester that lashed the sea into tumbling, angry foam. Found pussy willows by the way. The wind went down at sunset, and I walked home under a glorious full moon, which made beautiful the quiet fields and homesteads, the trees & dancing water. Tall, dry reeds shone like polished lances, & as I passed the swamp lands, a line of golden water followed me, rippling & shining.

May 1. Friday.

Abby & George Bangs left us yesterday and began housekeeping in their old home by the schoolhouse pond. I called on Abby today.

May 7. Thursday.

Walked at sunset by the pond, along Mayflower Bank. It was pleasant to tread the crisp, new grass and the dry elastic beds of moss & lichen. The evergreen vines (ground pine?) were silvering with age, thus belying their name. The pond was clear as crystal, and I could see below a long wide streak of white sand like a travelled highway, for over it tiny fish were constantly gliding. I found mayflowers, rosy & fragrant, under the rusty brown & green leaves that overran the bank.

May 11. Monday.

The green fields of Spring are beginning to be starred with dandelions. Brown hawthorn buds are swelling to green, syringa twigs are tipped with delicate green, lilac & rose leaves are unfolding, the peach trees show a faint pinkish tinge. The birds hold matin & vesper services, and at dusk, young frogs begin their sweet, shrill piping.

May 12. Tuesday.

Walked through the swamps with Alice Crosby, or rather around them, for the cranberry bogs are overflowed, and the water has crept through the thickets and encircled oak trees & slim white birches. We found pussy willows in abundance, some still in hoods of gray fur, others in thick plumy clusters of green or shimmering gray; and a few arbutus blossoms and delicate anemones.

May 13. Wednesday.

Ira Atherton came in noon train. At sun set, Steenie & I walked to the pine grove to hear the birds at their vespers.

May 14. Thursday.

Weather like June. I went mayflowering in the morning. Saw a great turtle drag his clumsy weight out from the tangle of cranberry vines, and swim easily across the pond. In the afternoon I went to the pines, spread a shawl on the brown pine needles & with "Christopher North" for pillow, lay there in perfect bliss for two hours. Birds flew over & near me, the sunlight stole through green branches, the pines murmured dreamily, and I lingered there until came a strong salt breeze from the sea whose dampness drove me home.

May 15. Friday.

A morning walk to Relief's. This walk is always a pleasure, tho' taken so often. The pines, – the swamps, – the quiet cemetery, – the square, yellow house, faded & weather stained, with quaint porch & front yard filled with fruit trees & old-fashioned posies, where live Sarah & Lucy Foster, – the tall rushes and alders and abundant wild-flowers, – and then the wide sea view and the peaceful quiet of Relief's darkened room, each in turn is full of interest. One queer little shed-like house, a little beyond the cross roads, has served in its time as dwelling-house, store, church-school house & granary, and is now the dwelling place of a misanthropic old man who after living with a good wife for thirty or forty years, has now religious scruples (!) as to the legality of their marriage, and puts the width of a field between himself & wife. She, like a second Griselda, trots over with his food three times a day in the foolish, forgiving affection of her heart. I suppose she thinks "The King can do no wrong."

May 17. Sunday.

After church, walked with Isa & Winnie to the shore, then around the pond. The sea was a dazzling silver gray, almost white. Some bright little dandelions had ventured down almost to the water line, seeming quite at home in the deep sand, & nodded a triumphant challenge to their kinfolk on the grassy cliffs above. We found arbutus, and violets blue & white, by the pond. The fields were red with sorrel, and the brook flowed over green water-cresses.

May 18. Monday.

Mother is better today. She has been in bed with acute rheumatism for a week. I gave the good doctor a nosegay of blue periwinkle from the garden bank to take home to his wife.

Visited Capt. Freeman's pines. In the heart of them is fenced in a square open place green with grass where grow a few wide-spreading fruit trees. The birds sing in the tall pines that surround it, and from the heart of the rosy peach blooms, the bees answer with their deep hum. It is a fragrant, sunny spot, and was always a bit of fairyland to my childish imagination.

May 19. Tuesday.

Found today green sprigs of money wort striped grass, coral spires of the sorrel, pretty green currant blossoms, milkweed, the pink & white of peach & cherry, & silver abele twigs, the small, velvety leaves just uncurling to silvery gray.

May 21. Thursday.

A rainy day. At 5 P.M. Win & I went to the pond, he with rod & I with basket. He caught one small fish, & I brought home mayflowers, violets, huckleberry blossoms, slender young ferns (one not yet unrolled from its curious compact little ball), and the leaves & buds of wild gooseberry, – all fresh & wet & shining from their shower bath. It is beautiful after rain. The water was gray & swift, dimpled by fast falling raindrops. A bobolink filled the air with bright music and a tiny yellow-bird made sunlight over the dark water & wet banks.

Nettie's Avenue

May 23. Saturday.

Isa left us this noon. – The avenues and orchard at Nettie's are at their loveliest. The fruit trees, their low branches often touching the ground, are fairy bowers of beauty & fragrance, every branch & twig strung thick with rose & pearl. The horse chestnuts are filling out their huge cones into whose green depths of shade it is so pleasant to gaze upward, and one maple shows a wealth of golden-green blossoms, as if it had been absorbing sunshine for months.

May 24. Sunday.

Oh, the grass! One could lie on its green couch for hours, gazing up through the silvery mist of abele foliage, watching the yellow-birds flash in & out of blossoming fruit trees, the homely spotted toad hop out from the grass to gaze at you with bright intent eyes, the lovely spring toilets of pansy & periwinkle, violet & dandelion; – and hearing the rustle of leaves, the wind in the pine trees, the hum of bees, cawing of crows, laughter of the bobolink and all the varied notes of robin, bluebird, cat-bird, pee wee, oriole, quail, sparrow, & swallow.

May 26. Tuesday.

The willows have at last cautiously put out green leaflets. I gather pansies & flowering almond, & sorrel from the red-veined fields. A delicious half hour I spent lying in the little flower garden.

May 28. Thursday.

I sit on the "throne" in our Castle and look out on the west meadow starred with dandelions, with gleaming flags like lances drawn up on either side the narrow ditch, and see the glow of sunset through the distant pine boles.

Walter took me out rowing this afternoon, & my vases are full of anemones, white violets, ferns, strawberry blossoms, buttercups & wild Solomon's seal from the thicket by the pond.

May 31. Sunday.

"Oh, the lovely, lovely May!" Apple & cherry boughs wreathed & garlanded with snowy bloom, and the horse chestnuts light lanes and avenues with their lantern-like flower clusters. These trees are like great beehives in shape, and standing beneath them we hear the deep continuous hum of bees overhead among the flowers. Dandelions are now tall & rank in aunt Nettie's orchard, but I like better the first golden darlings nestling in the grass. They already are going to seed.

June 1. Monday.

Rain today. I went over to the other house in midst of the pour, stood under the great chestnuts, quite sheltered from the rain pattering on my thickset green roof. In the evening Win & I called at Capt. Solomon Freeman's. Met his niece, Miss Georgie Freeman, an Illinois girl, whom we found very pleasant. Found Alice awaiting me, when we came home.

June 2. Tuesday.

Walked to Relief's. The poor girl has had another of her bad attacks (the last was four years ago) and could not speak or move hand & head. I chattered away to her, telling everything that I thought might interest her.

The sea was a lovely pale blue, and Relief's lane was bright with crane's bill geraniums and feathery dandelions gone to seed; and she loves it all, so dearly, and will never see it again. The old maids' house was half hidden by trees, great branches sweeping the balconied porch, and the orchard on its east side was full of apple blossoms.

June 8. Monday.

Mrs Copeland's funeral today. It was sad to think, when she was carried out of the doorway of her home for this last time, that not one of her name was left to hold the old homestead. She loved my mother, who has been like a daughter to her since Mary died, and to her Mrs Copeland has left the house, farm, and $1000. To me, she left $200.

The Badgers came tonight.

June 9. Tuesday.

"Gladness on wings, the bobolink, is here!" and his singing was the magnet that drew aunt Mame & her niece from their Castle this P.M. and over to the pines in search of the feathered musician. Find him? Of course not. He kept silence, perversely, until we were housed again, when he broke into sweet and saucy singing, as if laughing at us. We had a happy half hour in the grove, however, the soft lights & shadows playing on the carpet of pine needles and rough bark of the trees; and a ramble by the peat swamp, filling our hands with trembling birch leaves and blue flag flowers.

June 10. Wednesday.

Win took me to the West Brewster brook, tonight, but we were just half a day too late to see the herring caught. They shut down this morning for the last time. From May 15 to June 10 is the rule. Two or three fishermen were busy with a net, capturing some unlucky stray fish. Poor things! how they twisted about in the meshes of the net, and gasped & fluttered on the grass & sand until their pretty silvery sides were all stained with the brown earth. The Brook is a lovely, half-tamed creature, dancing through a grassy hollow between terraced hills, here spreading out into deep pools, there laughing and hurrying along over its stony path; now flashing foam from sudden little waterfalls, then swirling around the ruins of an old grist mill. On the hill behind the brook stands the Abraham Winslow house, long uninhabited and reputed haunted, and opposite this, with brook and road between, is a square mansion backed up against a hill, which has for guardians two magnificent silver abeles whose straight trunks, golden with lichen, rise free and unencumbered to a level with the house top, and then spread out in a thick canopy of silver gray. All about the brook, on the hillsides perch queer old houses, and here too, lie great rocks draped with green clinging vines.

Right: Haunted House

June 11. Thursday.

The hawthorn is in bloom, our little bush aglow with rosy color, & Mrs Pratt's hedge white and fragrant, sweetening the shady street.

June 13. Saturday.

Out early for flowers. The grass heavily silvered with dew, each grass blade strung with diamonds, rubies, emeralds, topaz, and I was soon as richly adorned with jewels as a princess, while low wet boughs of trees shook delicious little showers on my hair and face. I filled my hands with cypress vine, wild geranium, and spider wort deep purple and violet and white. The fields are white with daisies and golden with buttercups, and there are often great stretches of sweet blossoming clover. How I love the grass!

June 15. Monday.

Walked to Relief's. She is better & can talk to me again. Most beautiful to see & remember are the sweet purity of her face and her lovely, patient smile. – The sea was pale blue, and a light haze brooded over the water, through which gleamed the white spires & houses of the Cape towns over the Bay. The grassy road was jewelled with flowers, – buttercups, tiny bright cinquefoil, sorrel, wild geranium, blue flag, juicy clover, pretty blue-eyed grass, wild cherry, ferns. – I love to lie in the hammock under our silver abeles from sunset time until the light fades, the rosy hawthorn grows dim, the rustling silver above me turns to black, & the first star shines out from the gathering darkness.

June 16. Tuesday.

A ride in the woods this morning with Mrs Badger. The oaks were lovely in their fresh, shining leafage, & the wild lupine was in bloom, making purple patches on the open fields. Here and there it was so abundant as to color whole fields with its soft purple.

Our kitten & the swallows have had a frolic (?) this afternoon, Minnie crouching in the grass & springing vainly after the venturesome birds who wheeled in circles above her, swooping down within an inch of her nose, & darting from between her paws with a saucy note of triumph. Pretty sport to witness, but I would not have risked so much had I been a swallow.

June 18. Thursday.

Mr Badger left us for the Maine lakes, and aunt Mary went to Boston on the chance of getting up a successful petition for pardon for Eugene Darling, the prisoner in whom she is interested.

A wonderful sunset, the western sky burning with gold & rose color, and in the east a rainbow, the keystone of its arch lost in the clouds, but the rest clear & beautiful.

June 22. Monday.

Out rowing with Win in the morning. The pond blue & still, the sun heat intense, burning. We saw a huge bull frog & christened him "Maximus" with the spray from our oars. The little thicket by the pond – east shore – was cool & green & quiet, a tangle of brake, polygonatum [sic], low shrubs & trees, with here & there a brilliant flower to light up the green. The clover is in its glory, flooding the fields with color & fragrance. The white clover has petals like tiny butterflies poised on a leaf for flight.

At sunset Mrs Badger & I walked to the shore. Gathered fragrant bayberry & the wild pea which trails its purplish pink blossoms over the beach sand. The sea was wild & restless, filling the air with its complaining & the sea gulls soared & screamed above.

June 24. Wednesday.

Abby, George & little May Bangs spent the day with us.

June 27. Saturday.

Went ferning with aunt Dede in P.M. Aunt Mame & Frank Kilbourne came in evening train.

June 29. Monday.

Aunt Dede & Mr Holden returned to Boston today. Aunt Olive & Mr Winslow, Hattie & Mrs Burrill arrived. I like Mr Holden & his gentle ways. He is young in heart if old & feeble in body. We were good friends in a short time.

June 30. Tuesday.

The roses are superb, full-petalled and perfect, spicily fragrant, of every shade of red from the white tinged with faint color to deep & glowing crimson. Waterlilies have come & sway all day on the cool waves in Undine-like beauty. Crickets & frogs sing of nights, quails whistle in the long afternoons, and the sweet cut grass lies in windrows across the open fields.

July 2. Thursday.

Uncle Taylor, Albert & family came in evening train.

July 4. Saturday.

We met at breakfast, all wearing the red, white & blue. Mr Winslow had a huge bow for necktie & a coquettish red ribbon pinned to his white hair; aunt Mame wore the scarlet piano cloth over a blue & white dress; even mother wore the colors; the boys were in soldier rig; and I had a ribbon streamer fastened to one shoulder and a parti-colored cap on my head. After breakfast we sang & marched, shouted & laughed. Rendered the "Star Spangled Banner" to a piano, bell, & tin pan accompaniment, with waving of flags & handkerchiefs. After dinner, we went in procession to the other house, & sang patriotic songs to the music of piano & organ, violin & tambourine. In the evening, aunt Nettie & household came over here, also Octavia Crosby & little daughter, & Angie Crosby. Gracie Woodworth and Emmie Cobb appeared as Night and Morning. Gracie wore the crescent, & her dark eyes & hair were charming under her thin black veil spangled with stars. Emmie was lovely in white & pale blue draperies sprinkled with silver stars. May Bangs was a comet, with a long tail of pink Tarleton, her bright hair escaping from a silver band & hanging loose about her face. She darted about quite in her element; the role suited the young lady.

July 8. Wednesday.

The annual Union picnic in Cahoon's grove. I drove up with aunt Nettie & Lucy in the afternoon. Met the Nickerson girls – Priscie & Addie – for the first time since their arrival in Brewster, also Barnstable friends – Grace Howes, May Glover, Lizzie Monroe & Mamie Allen. Mr Holden sent me a great roll of songs today, & Fannie Tyler has invited me to visit her for two or three weeks next winter.

July 9. Thursday.

Nettie, Emily, Lucy, and the Nickerson girls here to tea. – Found white day lilies in Mrs Copeland's garden, very sweet & stately.

July 11. Saturday.

Lucy & Grace left in noon train. Mr Badger & Mrs Eaton came in eve.

July 20. Monday.

Annie Handy & I have agreed to study English literature & history together, sending each other once a week a list of twenty questions to be answered.

July 23. Thursday.

The Nickersons & our crowd went to Chatham, starting at 12.30, & reaching home at 9.15 P.M. We went by the South Orleans road, through the woods, coming out on a hilltop commanding a fine ocean view. Then we rode on through woods, past brown fields & ponds of blue, sparking water, & dreary treeless little graveyards, until Chatham came in sight. It has a pleasant village street with houses embowered in flowers & shrubbery. The great waves thunder on the sands, & white sails fleck the blue Atlantic. One hundred years ago, perhaps longer, the sea was a mile farther away, but one of the harbor bars gave way, & it swept in burying orchards & gardens & swamps in a deluge of sand. The bars are continually shifting, & now by reason of some change of the kind, the covering of sand is being swept off, & within a few months the greater part of an old orchard or swamp has been laid bare. We can see a curious peaty formation, deeply indented with footprints of men & little children & animals, & dotted with stumps of trees. An old well has also come to light, & the salt water dashes into it & dances about in glee. – I called on Susie Howard & she kept me to supper. She is a fine housekeeper & has a pretty little home. After tea, I joined my party at the hotel, & we rode home by moonlight, Mrs Thayer & myself singing all the way.

July 25. Saturday.

Went to look for "pussies" before breakfast, through the dew-wet fields where spider webs were glistening, over fences and ditches. The little soft gray things make lovely wreaths. – Library duties this afternoon. Went over to spend the night with Emily, Moonlight, & the little town looked weird, lovely & unsubstantial in the magic light!

Addie Nickerson and dog Foxell

July 26. Sunday.

Addie Nickerson called at sunset time. She is most attractive & lovable. – Our smoke tree is in full glory, – a soft mist through which the sun shines.

July 27. Monday.

Hattie & I took a tramp through the swamps. We filled our baskets with grasses, pink pokeweed, loose strife, meadow beauty, white elder flowers, wild red lilies and tiny white cranberry blossoms. We shall know where to find ripe blackberries in a week, & wild sugar grapes in the Fall.

32

July 28. Tuesday.

The Nickersons & ourselves went for a picnic in Cahoons Grove this afternoon. Had supper at sunset, & rode home by moonlight, which was pleasanter than an all day picnic. After supper we sat on a rude wooden platform overlooking the long reach of shadowy water. Long Pond is three miles in extent. The sunset light gleamed through the trees west of us, and the moon slowly rose through eastern clouds. We sat there long, singing hymns, patriotic songs, and negro melodies.

July 30. Thursday.

Annie Handy came in noon train. After tea, Frank Kilbourne offered us his horse & we went for a drive.

July 31. Friday.

Annie & I talked & sung & read over school letters in A.M. After dinner, Annie read "Miles Standish" aloud, while I sewed, & just before tea, Walter took us down to call on Relief. After tea, we played croquet with Mr Thayer & Mr Badger until it was too dark to see longer, then we all had a game of Rounce after which, Annie & I sat out on the front door step in the moonlight until 11 P.M.

August 1. Saturday.

Annie went with me to the Library. Miss Clara Baker came in & talked about the old times when my father was living & she was with us for a year as assistant teacher. She said my father was her ideal of a perfect gentleman. She still treasures a book containing many of his marks. She found me reading "Hiawatha" when about five years old, & said to me, "Why, Caro, what are you reading? You can't understand that!" I replied, "Not all of it, but I like the jingle of the words."

August 3. Monday.

Annie & I took the noon train, she to Barnstable, & I to Boston to do some writing for Albert. Found him awaiting me at Rutland Square, & he showed me what my work was to be.

August 5. Wednesday.

Ed Handy called this evening.

August 6. Thursday.

Went to Barnum's Hippodrome in afternoon with uncle Taylor.

August 8. Saturday.

A pouring rain. Task finished. Came home in morning train. Went to Library in P.M.

August 10. Monday.

Drove to Relief's & made a short call, leaving aunt Mame to spend the afternoon with her. Then Frank & I called on Abby Bangs.

August 19. Wednesday.

Emmie's birthday – nine years old.

August 20. Thursday.

Nettie, Emily, Mr Edes, aunt Mame, mother and I took tea at the Nickersons. Met Mrs Thomas Nickerson & her daughter Lily. We tried magnetism, & also what Priscie called a "literary & artistic" game. Good fun.

August 24. Monday.

Walked to Relief's. Gathered white asters, butter & eggs, golden tansy, dark elder berries, golden rod & cardinal flower. Autumn is already cooling the air, & hanging out bright tokens of the approaching carnival.

August 29. Saturday.

Winnie left us for Minneapolis.

August 30. Sunday.

Spent the morning with Relief. In eve called on our good Doctor Gould & wife. Their two sons came in, George & Charlie. Charlie, the elder, is home from a voyage. He is genial & warm-hearted. I liked his saying the other day at the Library, quite simply, before a number of us, that he "must go home, being man of all work just now; I peel potatoes, stone raisins, wipe dishes, do most anything that comes handy, to save my mother, steps."

August 31. Monday.

Steenie's fourteenth birthday. We decorated his room with flowers, grasses & wreaths, put new white coverings on bed & bureau, a birthday cake frosted & candied on one table, & his presents on another. He was so overcome with surprise & pleasure that he burst out crying and hid his face on mother's shoulder. He is a warm-hearted sensitive little fellow.

September 3. Thursday.

Frank & I drove over to Barnstable & spent the day with Annie Handy. Reached home at 8 P.M. Driving was rather nervous work the last half hour it was so dark.

September 4. Friday.

Gave aunt Nettie a surprise party this eve. We wore masks & appeared in costume. Mrs Thayer was a Normandy peasant girl, aunt Mame a Spanish duchess, Hattie a page, Steenie a Scotch laddie, Mr Badger a strong-minded old maid, Mr Thayer a courtier of Louis XIV's time, George Bangs a fashionable lady, & I was a nun. Addie Nickerson & Fanny Crosby came as street musicians, with violin and accordion. Their dress was gay & picturesque, & Fanny sung some charming ballads.

September 5. Saturday.

Baby Helen, Eliza Paine's only child, died last night.

September 8. Tuesday.

Ruth Paine came to us for flowers for the baby's funeral today.

September 9. Wednesday.

A party of us drove over to Scargo Hill in Dennis. An observatory has been built there, recently, & commands a fine view of the Cape, the ocean, & even Nantucket.

September 10. Thursday.

The Thayers went this noon.

September 12. Saturday.

Frank & Mr Badger went in morning train. Also mother & aunt Mame for a visit to Conway.

September 15. Tuesday.

I miss mother so much. The house seems empty & lonely. It is she who makes it home.

September 23. Wednesday.

Hattie & I rode up to our wood lot with George Bangs, & while he worked, we hunted for moss & lichen, explored wood paths etc. riding home on the load of wood in time for dinner. Mother was there, came in noon train, a joyful surprise.

September 24. Thursday.

A heavy dew this morning silvered the asparagus bushes, & hung on every leaf & blade of grass. The golden rod is abundant, in slender sprays, in thick & plu-my clusters, and asters, white & purple, star the fields. Bright alder berries light the roadsides, dogwood tempts us with its dangerous beauty, the reed grass waves its light brown plumes, & less plentiful is the darker beauty of the foxtail grasses.

September 29. Tuesday.

A driving easterly storm. Addie and Priscie, Lola Bangs, George, Emily, Grace and I drove to Nauset in the pelting wind & rain. It is a sandy, desolate place on the outside of the Cape, only one dwelling house & three light house towers. The ocean rolls and thunders at the base of the high sand cliffs, coming in in great rollers a translucent green as they slowly curve over to break into clouds of snowy foam, under cover of which the waves dash high up the beach. A "blinding mist came pouring down", and beyond the surf line we had glimpses only of the gray tossing waste of water.

September 30. Wednesday.

Mrs Eaton & Grace went in early train. Nell Atherton came. The wind blows a gale, the sea is black as ink, & many vessels are making for Provincetown harbor.

October 1. Thursday.

Walked through the swamps with Alice. We have had heavy frosts, but the trees are only beginning to change. Oak leaves are just edged with red & here & there is a single gold leaf on the birches, but the woodbine creepers are all aflame with color.

October 2. Friday.

Drove to the marshes this morning, & puzzled the little horse Fanny, by stopping for a long look at them. I love our marshes, and never tire of gazing at the beautiful levels, rich in color, in waving grasses, brilliant flowers, & winding creeks.

"Each change of storm or sunshine scatters free
On them its largess of variety,
For Nature with cheap means still works her wonders rare."

Nell, Hattie & I went to singing meeting this eve at the parsonage. The people meet there Friday evenings to practice congregational singing. We lingered after the meeting for a talk with Mr & Mrs Dawes.

October 5. Monday.

Went for a drive & brought home milk weed pods, just bursting open, disclosing their wonderful pearly white contents so closely packed, the dainty ovals held fast by the dark brown seeds. – Wonderful clouds today, heaped along the eastern horizon like a range of snowy Alps. – The garden is thinning fast. Nasturtiums, asters, French phlox, mignonette, balsams, marigolds, bloom on; a few sweet peas linger, but their pretty faces are touched by the frost, and a few late roses sweeten the frosty air.

October 8. Thursday.

The early sunlight slants across my page, (I am in the east parlor) and the cool morning wind plays the mischief with my hair. Out of doors, yellow leaves sail slowly down & mingle with the rustling masses under foot. Frost came in the night, and made a silver network of the asparagus, while trees & vines, & grass still fresh & green, glitter in the sunlight. – I hear that Jennie Comer, the frail anemone of the hospital, is dead, and patient little Maggie also. My pet Charlie is better, though he still makes sunshine in the hospital with his glancing golden curls. – Aunt Mame & I visited the old Sears house in the western part of the town, this afternoon. We followed the old stage road & after a long drive reached the house which is the oldest in town, and old in truth it looked, black & weather beaten, with great chimneys; a double house, with two front doors. Old David Sears, the owner, was alone & came to admit us, looking the very counterpart of Krook in "Bleak House," – old fur cap, spectacles, bristly chin, with a dog at his heels in place of the

Elijah Cobb House, East Parlor

cat; but his expression was far pleasanter, and he seemed bright & intelligent, in spite of his years. He is eighty-five. His great grandfather bought the place of one Judah Sears, & in his time it was a great farm with fifteen or twenty head of cattle, great hay harvests, & 250 bushels of corn at a husking. David's great grandfather, grandfather & father had all lived to be old men and died there, & he judged the house to be over 170 years old.

The rooms were low, with great central beams in ceiling, & the floors were much sunken in places. The great fireplace was closed up, but it must have been immense, with benches set in, from which one could look up chimney to the stars, and back logs eight feet in length. It kept one man busy all winter to supply the family with wood. We saw one fireplace like a small room, but this was not as large as the closed fireplace. A narrow door in the wall opened on a short flight of steps leading up to a tiny bedroom, a queer little nest of a place. A door in the kitchen opened on a narrow dark passage which led past a pantry and another little bedroom, to the old man's workshop.

38

October 13. Tuesday.

The golden leaves lie rustling underfoot, the woodbine creeps in & out of the lilac bush, & the vivid leaves like little tongues of flame wave triumphantly above it. The Nickerson girls came tonight to say good-bye. They go tomorrow.

October 15. Thursday.

Walked to Relief's & back. Each sunny day & cool night adds to the beauty of swamp & meadow. One large swamp was alive with the cranberry pickers, their odd dresses & sunbonnets dark against the red of the woods, & their bright tin measures glinting in the sunlight. Outside the swamp was drawn up a line of carts, filled with old coats & shawls, dinner-pails & baskets; the patient horses & oxen freed from these, were tethered to the rail fence. The sound of merry laughter & boyish shouts came to me pleasantly. Little Emmie Hall kept me company on the way home as far as the swamp where her mother was at work. She made a pretty picture, the small figure with a handkerchief tied over its brown curls, running in & out among the bright bushes.

October 16. Friday.

A long morning in the woods with Steenie. We drove through the woods & between two large ponds. The road lay across a narrow strip of land, bright with the autumnal beauty of trees & shrubs & alder berries, which separated the two ponds. On the right, the water rippled brightly on a narrow, sandy beach, & stretched wide & far away to a line of low sand cliffs misty in the distance. On the left was a smaller, shallower piece of water, red with the reflection of woods that crowded close to its margin, and near the shore spread with a network of lily leaves, silver in the sunshine, through which tall rushes pushed their way and red water grasses waved. A rising hill on whose summit stood an old brown wind-mill, gave the finishing touch to this picture. We left the carriage & walked past an old house, half hidden by pines & ancient apple trees with mossy trunks, its windows framed in climbing grape vines, to a high bluff covered with pines and affording a fine view of the water.

October 22. Thursday.

Drove to Scargo Hill, past the marshes, red, brown, purple & gold in the sunlight. We started a covey of quail feeding by the roadside & so near the color of earth & withered grass as to be barely visible.

It was a lovely Indian summer day, but too hazy for a clear distant view. We looked down on Scargo Lake, which was like a clear mirror reflecting the red & russet woods on the hillside.

October 24. Saturday.

Emily, aunt Mame & I sat up till 3 A.M. to see the eclipse of the moon. We made molasses candy to keep ourselves awake, and, as the hour approached, we went to the house top, & wrapped in blankets, lay back on cushions against the roof. It was wonderful, first the clear, white moonlight silvering the landscape, then the dark shadow of our earth creeping slowly over the bright disc (dark at first, then of a strange lurid hue) while gradually the pale stars grew bright, & myriads more became visible as the moon darkened. The hush & stillness of the night, the marvelous precision of our moving shadow recalled Addison's lines –

"What though in solemn silence,
all Roll round this dark terrestrial ball" etc.

We lay on the housetop until a white tide of mist, rising from the low lands and marshes, poured in upon & around us, driving us away. It was a strange sight, the waves of mist below gradually overwhelming meadow, wood, village and sea, even the constant light houses across the Bay, and above, the clear heaven and stars and veiled moon.

October 26. Monday.

Emily, aunt Mame & I drove to Dennis to visit the old Stone house. It was high tide and the marshes were overflowed, the tall reeds waving over blue, rippling water. When we returned, the tide had ebbed and the levels were bare and brown again. – The Stone mansion was large & roomy, set far back from the road. It was framed in oak and brought from Plymouth. We saw the original tiles over the fireplaces, & handsome old chairs, one of which was brought over from England by Nicholas Stone, and a great oil portrait of a family group, father, mother and two daughters; the mother a handsome middle aged lady in snowy cap or turban, dark satin dress, fine laces, gold chain and <u>immense</u> locket.

October 29. Thursday.

Nell Atherton left for Quincy.

40

November 1. Sunday.

Bessie Murphy went home, to our regret.

November 14. Saturday.

The first snow flakes are flying through the air. Yet I still find roses & sweet alyssum in aunt Nettie's garden, and one great chrysanthemum bush seems a little world in itself – of happy families, with its clusters of white & rosy flowers, large & small, all looking bright and fearless, in spite of cold winds. – We have sad news of two of our absent sea captains. Their ships, both loaded with coal, have been burned at sea, and the human freight tossed about on the stormy ocean for days, in the ships' boats. The crew of the Mogul – Capt. William Freeman, reached land in safety, but the Centaur lost part of the crew, and the young captain, Nathan Foster.

November 26. Thursday.

Thanksgiving day. Nine of us at dinner in the old homestead, Nettie, Emily, Walter, Emmie, Hattie Burrill, aunt Mary, mother, Steenie & myself. In eve, we put up a large gilt picture frame against a dark background, & had a few living pictures. Emmie was a demure little Evangeline in peasant costume, & also the little seamstress with Sydney Carton (myself) in the guillotine scene. – Later Nettie played. – Lohengrin and bits from Moscheles, Rubinstein & Mendelssohn.

December 2. Wednesday.

We were wakened at 2 A.M. by the loud ringing of the church bell, and a few minutes later, Emily burst in, hair & dress flying, exclaiming that Mrs William Freeman's house was again on fire, the second time within two weeks. We dressed hastily and ran over to the scene of confusion. The fire was within the walls, and the men were working steadily with axes & pails of water. It was an anxious time.

December 10. Thursday.

Walked to Relief's. The day mild & bright. I enjoyed the soft hissing of the wind through the yellow rushes. Black alder berries were bright against their gray leafless branches, and red-stemmed rosebushes made a line of color by the brook.

December 18. Friday.

A bright, windy day. The sea like one of Turner's pictures, great green rushing waves, tossing white caps high in air.

It is a sad Christmas season for the Fessendens. Ida, Ella & Huddie are dead, Bethia, & Florence Freeman are stricken with the same disease – typhoid fever.

Relief's Christmas is also dimmed in anticipation. Asenath is expecting to be confined every day, her first child after seven years of married life. Aside from the anxiety as to the issue, which is great, for Sene is far from strong, it must necessarily deprive Relief of her dear companionship for some weeks at least. Thomas is so good and thoughtful. He helps his wife with her sewing, evenings, by stitching for her on the machine.

The three faces were beautiful in different ways, yesterday: Relief's, pure & sweet in its soft whiteness, like a lily in the dark room; Asenath's like a waiting Madonna, her heavy waves of dark hair folded smoothly away from the low fair brow and quiet eyes; and Eliza's lovely in its sadness, but so changed from the dimpling brightness that bent over baby Helen a few weeks ago.

December 20. Sunday.

The snow falling in large, soft flakes, but my carol children came running through the snow & gathering darkness to practice for Christmas, Angie Crosby, tall & slender, with bright brown hair & handsome eyes, blue-eyed Lizzie _____? Rena Snow, quick and tiny and bright-faced, Charlie Crosby and Steenie, all with fresh, clear voices, singing heartily. – Asenath has her Christmas gift, a little daughter, born today.

December 23. Wednesday.

Hannah Snow's wedding day. She & Mr Collins left in the noon train for Boston, & tomorrow keep on to Laconia.

December 25. Friday.

Christmas Day. It dawned clear & fair, with a great, shining star in the east, and then full sunlight. In A.M. aunt Nettie drove to Relief's, carrying her many gifts, and playing to her some Christmas music. –

We sent a Christmas pudding to the Saint children, and Nettie carried pies & toys. She was received with beaming faces and chuckles of delight from the ragged youngsters. – A moonlight evening. The Hall bright with Christmas greens a happy faces, carols sung, poems recited, "Mrs Peck's Pudding" acted, speech & story from Mr Dawes, Santa Claus (George Bangs) with gifts for the children, supper & dance.

December 26. Saturday.

Singing meeting this eve at Nettie's, a double quartette practised for tomorrow. Tenors, Frank Kilbourne & Zoeth Snow; bassos George Bangs & John Clark; altos, Angie Crosby & Matilda Cobb; sopranos, Occa Crosby & myself.

December 27. Sunday.

Warm, sunny day – Christmas service. Sermon from text II Corinthians, IV-6 – "For God who commanded the light to shine out of darkness, hath shined in our hearts, to give the light of the knowledge of the glory of God in the face of Jesus Christ." The choir sung a carol "While shepherds watched their flocks by night," and the old joyous hymns "Brightest & best of the sons of the morning," "Joy to the world, the Lord is come!" and "Watchman, tell us of the night." I enjoyed singing with so many, & wish we might have a double quartette every Sunday. Our little minister was quite brimming over with pleasure at the singing and our Christmas zeal.

December 31. Thursday.

Have been busy sewing, getting ready for my Boston visit. Have read "Nicholas Nickleby" to Frank, & aunt Mame has read "Princess of Thule." Hattie Burrill left for Foxboro yesterday.

It is nearly twelve o'clock, & the year draws to a close. Goodbye to 1874. It has brought no sickness or sorrow to my dear home, and I have had many happy hours.

Books read in 1874

In Memoriam	Tennyson
Little Dorrit	Dickens
Hard Times	"
Martin Chuzzlewit	"
Les Miserables	Victor Hugo
A Message from the Sea	Dickens
Poems of Home & Travel	Bayard Taylor
The Cricket on the Hearth	Dickens
Pictures from Italy	"
The Cathedral	Lowell
The Chimes	Dickens
The Haunted Man	"
The Uncommercial Traveller	"
Boyhood of Great Men	[No author given]
Lectures on Literature & Life	Edwin Whipple
The Giaour	Byron
The Prisoner of Chillon	"
Walden	Thoreau
Views Afoot	Bayard Taylor
What to Wear	E.S. Phelps
A Week on the Concord & Merrimac Rivers	Thoreau
Our Mutual Friend	Dickens
Little People of the Snow	Bryant
In His Name	E.E. Hale
Villette	C. Bronte
Life of Dickens 3 vols.	Forster
Tam O'Shanter	Burns
The Brigs of Ayr	"
Yesterdays with Authors	J.T. Fields
A Chance Acquaintance	Howels
Ninety-Three	Victor Hugo
Lotus-Eating	George Curtis
Christopher North	Mrs Gordon
Thoreau: The Poet-Naturalist	W.E. Channing

Fireside Travels	Lowell
Bits of Talk	H.H.
Bits of Travel	" "
David Copperfield	Dickens
A Fable for Critics	Lowell
Their Wedding Journey	Howells
My Summer in a Garden	C.D. Warner
What Katy Did at School	Susan Coolidge
Army Life in a Black Regiment	Higginson
The Potiphar Papers	George Curtis
Anecdote Biographies of Thackeray & Dickens	Stoddard
Romola	George Eliot
Malbone: an Oldport Romance	Higginson
A Brave Lady	D.M. Muloch
Sir Rohan's Ghost	Harriet P. Spofford
Azarian	" " "
The Four Georges	Thackeray
Marjorie Daw	T.B. Aldrich
Suburban Sketches	Howells
Prudence Palfrey	Aldrich
Kavanagh	Longfellow
Out-Door Papers	Higginson
Maud	Tennyson
The Old Woman Who Lived in a Shoe	Amanda Douglas
The Tone Masters. Mozart & Mendelssohn	Charles Barnard
" " " Handel & Haydn	" "
" " " Bach & Beethoven	" "
The Best of all Good Company	Blanchard Jerrold
The Newcomes	Thackeray
Dreamthorpe	Alex. Smith
Katherine Earle	Adeline Trafton
Venetian Life	Howells
A Foregone Conclusion	"
Princess of Thule	Wm. Black
Christmas Carol	Dickens

Mother and Daughter
Helen Cobb Dugan and Caroline Atherton Dugan

1875

January 2. Saturday.

A rainy day. Aunt Mame & Frank went to Boston in noon train.

January 5. Tuesday.

A still, cold day, the landscape all in gray and white as if photographed. I drove down for a goodbye call on Relief.

January 6. Wednesday.

We closed the house, & mother & I took the noon train for Boston. I left the train at Bridgewater, and walked up the familiar street. Miss Woodward came to meet me & walked with me to the Briggs's. Mrs Briggs gave me a cordial welcome. After supper I went to Normal Hall & spent the eve with Miss Woodward. It was good to see her, the soft waves of gray hair, the strong, sweet face, the kindly gray eyes and the beautiful spirit shining through them. Dear Mother of the School, how much we owe to her! I read aloud Longfellow's "Hanging of the Crane," & she read to me her favorite bits of "Snow-Bound," & we looked over pictures & photographs, & she showed me her books & plants. Mr Briggs called for me later.

January 7. Thursday.

An early breakfast. Snow falling fast. At 8 o'clock I said goodbye to the Briggs, went to Normal Hall for a half hour with Miss Woodward. She gave me a photograph of herself which I like much. I bade her goodbye & took the train to Boston, & Fannie Tyler, who gave me a warm welcome. Lizzie Longley from Northampton, came to tea. She is a pretty, pleasant girl and a sweet singer.

January 9. Saturday.

Snowing, but I sallied out & called on Abby Adams at the Bigelow School, South Boston.

January 10. Sunday.

To Hollis St. church in A.M. where I met aunt Mame & Frank. In P.M. went with Lizzie Longley to vesper service at Mr Hale's, Union Park St.

January 11. Monday.

Lizzie Longley & I went with Mr Tyler this evening to the Boston Theatre, to see bright little Lotta in "Musette."

January 14. Thursday.

Mother spent the day here.

January 15. Friday.

Steenie came in & went down town with me. He said "You do look handsome, sister. If I wasn't your brother, I should marry you!" We visited Williams [sic] & Everett's, and dined at cousin Albert's.

January 20. Wednesday.

I met aunt Mame & we went to the Mass. Historical Rooms. These are not open to the public, as they belong to a private association of about one hundred members, but aunt Mame had a letter of introduction, and we were received with kindness & courtesy, and shown through the rooms, eight in all. We saw many books, pictures & relics. The swords of Miles Standish, Governor Carver, and Sir William Pepperell, Franklin's court suit, worn in France, the "Mayflower" Bible, Prescott's slate for writing & the original M.S. of "Conquest of Mexico," Washington's epaulets, plain gold, worn at siege of Yorktown, Paul Revere's pistol, said to have been carried on the night of his memorable ride. In one of the rooms we saw a pair of unfinished slippers picked up in Baltimore, black velvet on which was embroidered the Confederate flag, the work of some Southern woman for brother or lover. In another was a great, brass handled chest of drawers from Salem, of which the legend is that a witch once sprang out of one of the drawers, for which feat of agility she was hung on Gallows Hill. We saw a leaf torn from the Bible by a witch while Cotton Mather was preaching, & there is his own handwriting in proof! Also an immense hinge from Andersonville prison, & six of the pieces of wood that formed its "dead line."

January 25. Monday.

A cold has kept me housed since last Wednesday. The days have passed quietly and pleasantly in singing and sewing, playing parcheesi [sic], talking with Fannie and reading aloud to her H.H's "Bits of Travel."

January 27. Wednesday.

To the Children's Hospital this morning. Saw sweet-faced Sister Theresa.

Will Hovey, the new editor of the Transcript, and his bright little wife Fannie, were here to tea.

January 30. Saturday.

Mother, Steenie & I spent the day with the Badgers. Mr Badger has a fine library.

February 2. Tuesday.

Aunt Dede & I spent the afternoon at Mt. Pleasant with Mrs Daniells. I played cribbage with Minnie Daniells. She is very deaf & attends the deaf mute school, is a child for her years, - all the result of scarlet fever. She is very sweet and patient.

February 4. Thursday.

Nell Greely dined here. She is slender and quick-motioned, with dark, laughing eyes and light hair. I liked her at once, and enjoyed her fine singing. – Edward Handy called and spent the eve.

February 6. Saturday.

Spent the day at Blind Institution, and by so doing missed calls from Miss Woodward, Abby Adams, Emmie, Harriet & Emily. Minnie Tyler came tonight.

February 8. Monday.

Nell Peterson was here for three hours. She is thin and delicate looking after her long illness. She still wears her auburn hair in soft loose curls, and out of her earnest blue eyes looks the Nell of old times. She is coming as assistant book keeper to Dr. Howe. Carrie French, a next door neighbor, was here to dinner, a plain, deformed little body, but sweet and lovable. – This evening, Minnie and I went with Mr Tyler, on Col. Holbrook's invitation, to see Mrs Jarley's Wax-Works at the St. James Hotel. The Colonel has beautiful rooms there.

February 9. Tuesday.

Minnie & I have been looking over Fannie's jewel box - garnets, malachite, pearls, emeralds, diamonds. Fannie gave me a pair of ear-rings of Bohemian garnet.

February 10. Wednesday.

Nell Greely came over to dinner. In half an hour appeared a lovely bouquet & a letter from her friend Kitty Morse, from whom she had just parted down town. Kitty fell in love with little Nell from just seeing her on the street, wrote to her & then called to take her to ride. Now she is Nell's devoted cavalier, sees her daily, takes her to ride, always escorts her into Boston, keeps her constantly supplied with music and flowers, and is quite fiercely jealous of her.

February 11. Thursday.

Snow & rain. Mr & Mrs Loring Barnes, Fanny and Howard here to tea. Mr B. is the president of the Handel & Haydn Society. Nell sung.

February 12. Friday.

Nell went home. She is charming, with her gift of song, her slender little figure, dancing dark eyes & sunny hair. "Little tow head," Fannie laughingly calls her. – Minnie Tyler & I visited the German Catholic Cathedral today.

February 13. Saturday.

Minnie spent last night with the Greelys & returned today with the news that little Nell had broken her collar bone. She ran down the steps last eve to speak to Kitty Morse, and slipped and fell on the ice.

February 14. Sunday.

Sent a note & valentine to Nell, by Philip Greely, who was here to tea.

February 16. Tuesday.

Aunt Dede & I had our pictures taken at Hazleton's today. I had a letter from H.H.! [Helen Hunt Jackson]

February 18. Thursday.

Fannie Barnes sent in two tickets for the symphony concert, & I asked Nettie to go with me. We heard Schumann's "Paradise & the Peri," given for the first time in Boston, with Mr Lang as conductor.

February 23. Tuesday.

Went to Cambridge to see the little "Lorelei." Nell has a pretty room, & was a picture herself, her golden hair & dark eyes against the white pillows.

February 26. Friday.

Out again to see Nell & take her some fruit. Her room was sweet with flowers, rosebuds, camellias, English violets & calla lilies.

February 27. Saturday.

Nell Peterson snowed down on the door-step just night, & right glad was I to see her. We had a pleasant evening, talking & laughing over old times.

February 28. Sunday.

Nell P. and I spent a quiet day at home. The wind whirled the fine particles of snow about, till the air was full of the waving and glittering as of a magic veil, shot through with sunshine. – I finished up the winter by spraining my ankle this afternoon. I was writing a note to Nell Greely and rose to reach a penwiper. My right foot was dead asleep & twisted & bent, landing me on the floor & in a minute I was faint with the pain. I managed to hop down to supper and it did not pain me much in the evening. Gave my note to Philip to take to Nell. Mr Holden, Nell P. and I discussed Dr. Howe, Chas. Sumner, prison systems, capital punishment, murder, guillotine, &c, [This is Caro's sign for etc.] curious topics for Sunday night!

March 1. Monday.

Ankle badly swollen & very painful. Dr. Jackson called in. No bones displaced but a bad sprain. Must not put it to the floor for a week. I spent the day on sofa in Frank's room. Gertie Bigelow called.

March 2. Tuesday.

Spent the day in Mr Holden's room. Mr Tyler came up to see me in eve.

March 5. Friday.

Mother & Nettie came to see me. Mother has been in Lunenburg, with Steenie.

March 6. Saturday.

Aunt Mame & Steenie came to see me. I cannot walk yet, tho' my foot is better. Fannie Hovey called & promised to take me to see Janauschek, if I am able.

March 10. Wednesday.

Fannie Hovey & her little Jennie here to spend the day. Kitty Morse drove in town bringing little Nell. They did not come in, but Frank and I went to the door. I liked Kitty, she has such a fresh, bright face, and a gay, off-hand manner. – Later, May Greely called.

March 11. Thursday.

The Barnes's - Fanny & her father & mother - called this eve. Mr B. is fine looking, gray hair, deep voice and hearty laugh. Mrs B. has a pleasant plain face & a quick, crisp, amusing way of talking, Fannie is rather pretty & interesting, with little pettish, spoiled-child ways. - Lizzie Crotty came to invite me to a Cape Cod party at Mrs Badger's tomorrow eve, which of course I cannot attend.

March 12. Thursday.
[Should be Friday]

I went in to see Carrie French, at sunset.

March 13. Friday.
[Should be Saturday]

Steenie came, bringing me flowers - sweet alyssum, smilax & a love-ly rosebud. He is a dear, devoted little cavalier.

March 16. Tuesday.

Mother called this morning, looking very lovely with her gray hair in wavy crimps. Azubah French called. She is an independent, bright, odd piece of humanity. Also Lizzie Longley.

March 18. Thursday.

Fanny Barnes sent me two tickets for the Symphony concert today, & I invited Nettie to go with me; and we did enjoy it.

March 19. Friday.

Marie Johnson has been here - the charming little Marie who was fellow passenger with Frank in the Ville de Paris in 1869. She is a niece of Father Lyndon, a Catholic priest of Boston, and was then on her way to be educated at a convent in Brussels. She was so homesick there that the Lady Mother sent her home to America. She is now Madame Emile Souloumiac, having married a young French physician two years ago. She has crossed the Atlantic six times since 1869, and was wrecked in L'Europe, and taken off by the Greece. She was three years in a convent school, and married before her husband had graduated, but in a short time came home because she "took his mind from his studies." No wonder! She has the sweetest, most bewitching face, and charming manners and tact. She is very French, with a delightful accent. "Were you not very lonely for your daughter?" she asked Mr Holden.

Augusta Mayo came to spend a few days.

March 20. Saturday.

Mrs Hovey sent tickets for Janauschek, as she could not go, and I invited Fanny Barnes. Janauschek was fine as Mary Stuart, and most queenly in her sweeping black robes. She was charming also in the comedy of "Come Here."

In the evening, Frank had a little company, the Barnes' and Hoveys, Lizzie Longley, Nettie, Emily & Walter, Augusta read, and we had music. Augusta looked well, in black silk, white lace tie, & a touch of bright color.

March 22. Monday.

Steenie went to the Cape. Mother here to dinner. Half an hour before dinner, in danced little Nell, with her arm in a sling. Kitty Morse came for her at 4 P.M. Abby Adams called.

March 23. Tuesday.

Aunt Mame & I went to Crosby & Nichols', and Estes & Lauriat's to look at books, then to Cambridge & called on Mrs James, Lizzie Munroe & Mamie Allen. Then I went to see Nell and May Greely.

March 25. Thursday.

My last day here. Called on Annie Richardson and Carrie French, &

packed my trunk. Lizzie Longley came in & sang to me. A quiet evening. Played parcheesi with Mr Holden & Frank.

March 26. Friday.

My twenty-second birthday. Gifts from mother, Steenie, aunt Mame, aunt Dede and Frank Tyler. Left 330 Shawmut Ave. at 7.30 A.M. The bright faces of Effie & Julia looked after me from the window. Frank stood on the doorstep and behind her was aunt Dede, and Mr Holden's white beard. Frank's last words were "Tell your mother and aunt Mary if they will give you up, I want to adopt you." Saw Abby Adams at the station, en route for Bridgewater. Mother & aunt Mame appeared & the car ride did not seem long. Steenie met us with the carriage and we rode home facing a strong sea breeze, over roads so bad we were literally showered with mud & snow. Found little black Teddy (the kitten) on the doorstep to welcome us, and Mrs Mullen in the house which was already warm and comfortable, with three great fires. How desolate the dear home has been all winter! I am glad to return, to let air and sunshine into the rooms, and break the silence with merry voices and laughter and snatches of song. We had a jolly time unpacking silver & setting the table. Nothing in the house to eat save a few tongue sandwiches that Frank had put up for me, so Steenie went over to Joanna, & returned with a basket full of dinner. We unpacked, dusted, made beds, &c. and this eve I have been writing to Frank.

March 27. Saturday.

A busy day. Steenie brought down crutches from the "Estate" and I was glad enough of them. Alice Crosby called, & was pleased with the fan I brought her.

March 31. Wednesday.

After four weeks of snowdrifts and cutting winds, March is bidding us farewell as benignly & brightly as if he had been always the most genial of companions. Wild geese are flying northward, robins are here, and the leafless orchard is alive with blackbirds in full song.

April 1. Thursday.

A gray sky, pale gleams of sunlight, and a rushing wind. No sounds save the occasional "caw, caw" of some distant crow.

April 5. Monday.

A steady, fine rain. Steenie brought me a great piece of bark, covered with golden lichen, & tiny cups of gray & yellow, - lovely in the sunlight.

April 6. Tuesday.

Read some of my father's letters to my mother in the second year of their marriage. Also some of grandma's & grandpa's love letters, quaint & formal in form, but showing the love later made manifest in their wedded life.

April 7. Wednesday.

Sunny & mild. Aunt Mame, Steenie & I spent two hours on the front doorstep this morning, listening to the birds and (S. & I) playing Parcheesi.

April 21. Wednesday.

Nettie & Emmie came home.

April 23. Friday.

To drive with Nettie. What pleasure to breathe the mild, fresh air! The grass is springing, crocuses open their deep richly tinted cups, and mayflowers begin to show.

April 30. Friday.

A drive in the woods with Nettie. The open fields were rich in mosses of gray green and silvery hues, with here and there a patch of darker, purplish briar stems or poverty grass for contrast.

Steenie has the measles, and is a sick child, tho' we trust the worst is over.

May 1. Saturday.

A gray May Day. The best cheer is indoors, where a wood fire crackles on the broad hearth, crocuses, daffodils, mayflowers fill the vases, the west window is bright with plants in blossom, and mother dear makes another window bright with her presence. - I am reading "Little Women" to Steenie.

May 2. Sunday.

Rode to Relief's, my first call since my return. Nettie played & I sang.

May 7. Friday.

The Sears's, Martha Huckins & Susie Howard here to tea.

May 10. Monday.

Sat at my open window all the morning making Relief's May basket. A strong wind is sweeping in from the sea, and sounding in the tree tops, the kind that aunt Mame and I call a Beethoven wind. Aunt M. is raking the yard in a gay costume of balmoral, scarlet jacket & big "flat." I long to go & do likewise, but my crutches, like familiar spirits, lean against my chair, and remind me that I am a prisoner.

May 11. Tuesday.

Again at my window in the early sunshine that sweetens breakfast wonderfully. A pretty sight is outside. From the topmost twigs of the snowberry bush under my window to the grass below passes & repasses little flashes of red, blue & amethystine light. It is like a fairy kaleidoscope, but closer inspection finds them to be tiny drops of dew strung on invisible threads of spider web, & colored by the sun. - Relief has her May basket this afternoon. It was made of mosses, green, gold & gray, and tree lichen, & held gifts from Nettie, mother, Steenie, aunt Mame & myself. Mother contributed a lovely old-fashioned wine glass, stamped with a gold flower. Aunt Mame carried the basket and spent the afternoon with Relief, who was delighted with her May gifts, and sent me a lovely tea rose for thanks.

May 14. Friday.

I made my crutches carry me about the yard & garden this morning, but was tired after it. It is not easy to walk with crutches. My ankle is no better, & the more I favor it, the more exacting it becomes. I am overwhelmed with the kindness of friends & acquaintances, - grandsires, matrons, old & young, Irish and all, - who condole with me, comfort me with cheerful accounts of persons who were laid up one, two, even four years with sprained ankles, and advise, each a different remedy, which is guaranteed a sure cure. If my foot had been treated to all that has been recommended - arnica, rum and saleratus, catholicon, wormwood and rum, arnica blossoms, sea water, rum & salt, salt & water, beef pickle, potato water, brandy, balsam liniment, sweet oil & camphor, &c., it would have been washed quite away! I tried the first four "sure cures," then ceased experimenting, & now confine myself to the last which Dr. Gould prescribed. –Yesterday, I was hailed from the road with the inevitable two questions: "Well, Miss Caro, how is your foot today? - What are you doing for it?" I reply, & listen to a long eulogy on Streeter's Liniment, (inwardly resolving <u>never</u> to use it, ungrateful creature that I am!) and good old Captain Solomon drives off, his duty done. Unfortunately, he is one who likes to make sure of the working of his remedies, so I rather dread his next appearance.

May 17. Monday.

"Janet-donkeys!" is at present the family cry. The yard is newly seeded, young grass springing, and butchers, fruit men, neighbors, &c. persist in driving up on our cherished green. I shout Miss Betsey's warning cry whenever a vehicle approaches, & mother dashes to the rescue. Then follows a brisk war of words, & the intruder departs. This morning a white-topped cart appeared on the scene, & out went mother, - a lively Betsey Trotwood II. After some vigorous talk and a little trade, the encounter ended as follows:

Butcher: - "Shall you have a houseful this summer?"
B.T. II: - "Oh, I don't know; I may die before summer."
Butcher, with concern: - "Be you poorly?"
B.J. II: - "Certainly. Don't I look thin?"
Butcher chuckles - can't help it.
B.J. II: - "Afraid of losing one of your best customers, are you?
Well then, don't you drive up on my green again, or I shall die of a broken heart!"
Butcher drives off, still chuckling.

May 19. Wednesday.

Evening. The fire blazes on the hearth, and a Viking of a sea-wind is marching around the house & shouting down the chimney. I enjoy it, for I love our wild winds. - The mornings are sweet and sunny as heart could wish, but every afternoon comes a sea breeze to rollick over the land.

May 22. Saturday.

Drove over to spend Sunday with Nettie. A wealth of green & fresh foliage; meadows gay with dandelions; violets hiding in wet places; fruit trees in white & rose color.

May 24. Monday.

Emily came at noon, in excellent spirits. Mother drove to Harwich with Captain Freeman & spent the day with Hattie Brooks. I came home from Nettie's, to find old Joshua Dillingham here to tea, (altho' he had said he had "no occasion for it") and discussing old houses with aunt Mame.

Caroline Atherton Dugan

May 25. Tuesday.

The Sunday School children have had a picnic in Capt. Solomon Freeman's grove, and have just gone home. The sky is gray now, drops of rain are falling, the wind sighs in the trees and comes to me laden with fragrance of sweet briar.

June 13. Sunday.

Nearly three weeks since I have written in my journal. I am back in the "castle," my dear room, with its roof like a white tent, its old-fashioned furnishings, its sunset window, my books and pictures and wild flowers in the vases. It is good to be here again. We have a larger family - aunt Dede & Mr Holden, Hattie & Mrs Burrill, aunt Olive and Mr Winslow. My ankle is incased in a starched bandage four or five yards long, which acts as a splint, & I can walk with comparative ease without crutches.

June 16. Wednesday.

The Stallknechts have come, and we like them. Mrs S. is lovely in person & character; Josie (Josepha Victoria Rauscher Stallknecht) is an exceedingly pretty little girl; Charlie, aged six, is a dear, sturdy boy; and Harry, seventeen and standing over six feet in his stockings, is manly & merry & courteous. Thorwald and the father will come later.

June 17. Thursday.

Our church bell rang in the day at 3 A.M. We were busy with costume-making in the morning, for Nettie had invited us to a centennial tea party in afternoon. About 4 P.M. we began to assemble on the lawn. The dress of each new comer was greeted with merry shouts - a novel salutation, cocked hats and white satin gowns, epaulets & high combs, buff vests & white caps, curls & cockade appeared in turn. We played tag, & hide and seek with the children, & had supper at a long table out of doors. Then we adjourned to the house for music, dancing and games, & then, Mr Dawes read to us the speeches in Music Hall – the welcome of Massachusetts, and of Boston to our sister States of the South, through the words of Governor Gaston & Mayor Cobb, and the fine response of Lee and Andrews for Virginia and South Carolina. Our little minister's voice trembled with emotion, as he read of Lee & Kilpatrick standing with clasped hands under the old flag.

June 18. Friday.

Yesterday was a day of days in Boston! The boys in blue & boys in gray marching side by side through its streets in peace and goodwill, with every step trampling underfoot the bitterness & hatred engendered by civil strife; the glory of our colors overhead; the happy faces below; the storm of cheering from thousands & thousands of throats! And only ten years after the war!

June 21. Monday.

It is like a bit of the millennium! The beautiful tribute of the Fifth Maryland to our Federal dead; the sincere & earnest expression of repentance from Baltimore; the words of that sightless soldier to Gen. Lee - "General, your boys put my eyes out, but I am glad to see you here in our midst"; the universal good feeling and brotherly love.

June 23. Wednesday.

Unitarian Conference here and Mr Hale preached.

July 19. Monday.

A pleasant summer. I enjoy our houseful of boys. Harry Stallknecht, the eldest is full of fun & frankness; his brother Thorwald is a quiet, handsome boy of thirteen with warm heart & quick temper; Fred Wilde, chum of the latter, is merry and bright & a little gentleman - "a sweet boy if he <u>has</u> got red hair" as Harry had told me beforehand; Charlie is a manly little fellow of quaint speech & dignity; there are my brothers, Theo, the "yellow-haired laddie," lately returned from Minneapolis, and Steenie, my devoted cavalier; and at the other house are Walter & his friend Harry Badger.

We have two roly-poly little kittens named Demi & Daisy, and Charlie is devoted to them.

July 20. Tuesday.

I am reading stories-diaries-histories relating to our Civil War, moved thereto by the late Centennials. My personal memories are only of fairs in aid of our soldiers, in which my childish fingers tried to assist; of seeing a few Massachusetts regiments on Boston Common, start off for Washington; of the rejoicing when the war was over; of the darkness of sorrow over Lincoln's death.

August 28. Saturday.

A picnic at Greenland Pond, the picnickers being the Nickersons, Bangs's, Sears's, aunt Nettie's household, Theo, Steenie, Hattie & myself. Cora Nickerson looked like a little German Gretchen, with her rosy face, blue eyes, & thick fair hair in long braids. The woods showed bits of autumn color. We rowed on the lovely sparking water, had a clambake in a little grapevine arbor, dinner on the grass, & Emily read aloud Harriet Prescott Spofford's "Ray," a pathetic war story, while we made wreaths of oak leaves, golden rod & clethra.

August 30. Monday.

The Stallknechts went this morning. Goodbye to my little Charlie. What shall I do without him? No eager little hands to gather "slippers" for me; no active feet to mount the Castle stairs half a dozen times daily, bringing their owner into my lap for a little talk; no merry eyes to laugh back into mine; no sturdy little figure to march beside me in my walks. I miss the quaint child talk already, the loving kisses, the goodnight talk after Charlie is in bed waiting for the sand man to come.

He brought me his two clay pipes as a parting gift, saying "You may want to blow bubbles, Miss Caro," and his grief at leaving me was such that he could not come out to the dinner table, but watered his solitary meal with tears in his own room.

September 2. Thursday.

The house seems very empty, all because of the absence of one small man. No one to be undertaker at the chickens funerals; to use bow & arrow; to make eel spearers and kites; to eat mother's little round cookies; to tuck away the kittens Demi and Daisy, in his loose sailor shirt, like a 'possum; to help sprinkle clothes; to watch for woodchucks; to play "boat" in the hammock and row me to New York and Denmark. I must not forget his calling Demi & Daisy "little circus kittens" when they climbed the grapevine out of reach, or his being "asperated" with Steenie and saying he had "got into a nice little mess," and "Harry took me into the house and laid me on my stomach on the bed, and took up the hair-brush, and don't you s'pose I knew what he wanted?"

Charlie's mother told me of a dream of his, just after his playmate, their gardner's little daughter, died. He thought an angel came and told him Mamie wanted him, and he nestled under the great white wings - so soft and warm! - and flew away to heaven; and there he saw Mamie, and God was making puppy dogs and He showed Charlie how. Told in his earnest, grave fashion, his dream gave his mother an involuntary pang.

September 13. Monday.

Relief's twenty-ninth birthday.

November 19. Friday.

Annie Handy came to spend a few days with me.

December 24. Friday.

Christmas Eve! I have been reading the "Carol" to Frank Kilbourne. He came with aunt Mame last night, and Emily & Walter came tonight. E. went up to attend uncle Taylor's funeral. His death makes a sad Christmas for Albert. Steenie went over to welcome Walter and returned with a basket-ful of Christmas packages, wild with excitement, having witnessed the opening of gifts at the other house. There was nothing for it but to follow suit, and soon the Middle room was a scene of merry confusion, the piano covered with gifts, & the floor strewn with wrapping papers. Among my gifts was a fine photograph of George Harris, and best of all, a little note of reconciliation from Henry. When I learn through Julia Boylan, that this was what George wanted & tried to bring about a year ago, I realize what a dear, true, generous friend has vanished from earth. The memory of his brave cheerfulness, his generous, loving heart, his ready sympathy and help will live on in the hearts of his friends.

Elijah Cobb House, Middle Room

December 25. Saturday.

We kept Christmas day at the old house, Nettie, Emily, & the children coming over for the day. We had the Christmas dinner, games and singing. Walter & Frank carried our gifts to Relief, to my friend Alice, to Bessie Murphy and little lame Maggie. A quiet day, but very pleasant.

December 29. Wednesday.

Tonight, the children came to practice carols for the New Year party, singing "Happy New Year" under my window before coming in, a bright, interesting set of children.

Books read in 1875

Hanging of the Crane	Longfellow
Blind pits	[no author given]
Italian Journeys	Howells
Bits of Travel	H.H.
Our New Crusade	E. E. Hale
The Gayworthys	A. D. T. Whitney
Alton Locke	Charles Kingsley
Among the Isles of Shoals	Celia Thaxter
The Fair God	Lew Wallace
Homes of the New World	Fredrika Bremer
Pilgrim's Progress	Bunyan
The Improvisatore	Andersen
Northern Travel	Bayard Taylor
Henry Esmond	Thackeray
The Virginians	"
The Cenci	Shelley
Prometheus Unbound	"
A Norseman's Pilgrimage	Boyesen
St. George and St. Michael	MacDonald
Oldport Days	Higginson
Among the Pines	Edmund Kirke
My Diary North and South	W. Russell
Youths Hist. of the Rebellion	Thayer
Story of the Guard	Jessie Fremont
The Drummer Boy	Trowbridge
America before Europe	Count de Gasparini
Hospital Sketches	Louisa Alcott
Massachusetts in the Civil War	Schouler
Christmas Carol	Dickens

1876

January 1. Saturday.

The children had a New Year party at the Hall tonight. Tableaux, dialogues, carols, supper, games. Mr Dawes talked to the little folks in his usual happy fashion, & read to their elders, Tennyson's "Ring out, wild bells, to the wild sky." Little May Bangs was a lovely "New Year," in misty white, her earnest little face framed in the red gold of her flowing hair, and a branch of green pine in her outstretched hand. Rena and little Warren Snow have sweet faces, like the pictures of child angels. Our Emmie was also charming, with her rich coloring and radiant eyes.

January 3. Monday.

Last night, Capt. William Lowe Foster hung himself. He was at the Hall on Sat. eve, looking on at the happy play of the children.

Nettie, Emily, little Em, and Frank Kilbourne left for Boston this noon. Now we shall settle down for the winter.

January 4. Tuesday.

Such a sunrise! Pink clouds & clear golden light in the east, the zenith one flush of rose color, and in the west a great blue gray banner through whose rents shot red gleams of light. This year has had a beautiful opening, days mild & hazy and golden as Indian summer, with wonderful sunrises and sunsets. Today, we have a north wind that beats the sea into foam, waltzes with the trees and shakes the windows.

January 8. Saturday.

A long day at the Library arranging books. Election of officers for the year, in P.M. President, Mrs Elijah Knowles; Vice Pres. Martha Huckins; Sec'y & Treasurer, Ida Winslow; Managers, Melissa Foster & Sophie Hopkins; Librarian, Caro A. Dugan.

March 3. Friday.

I have been busy for two weeks helping about an entertainment for benefit of our Ladies Library, which took place this eve. It was a clear, moonlight night, & Knowles's Hall was packed with people. We had a supper of baked beans, brown bread, doughnuts, &c., music, tableaux, and a play "The Old-fashioned Kitchen" in which Mr Coffin and I took the parts of an old farmer and his wife, with seven children. Among the tableaux was "John Alden's Courtship" (with Glover for Alden and Nellie Lincoln for Priscilla), and scenes from "Lady Wentworth," Mr Asaph Crosby being the Governor, John Clark the Parson, and Laura Baker - Martha Hilton. In the first scene, Emily Lincoln was a capital Dame Stavers, and bright-faced Lily Crosby was the little Martha. Many of the audience were in costume, some charming, some grotesque. Mother wore an ancient green satin gown, with wide lace frills in the drapery sleeves and a white Martha Washington cap. Alice Crosby said to her, in a simple, honest, surprised way, "Why, I don't see as you look very old-fashioned, Mrs Dugan; you look pretty!" - Ida Winslow was pretty in figured silk & close cottage bonnet of white with cherry ribbons. Her sister Emma was quite magnificent in lavender brocade. Laura Baker wore bridal white, a quaint satin gown, bonnet & long lace veil, and with her fair face and simply dressed hair, looked as if she had stepped out of some old picture frame.

March 6. Monday.

Alice and I took train for Boston. I stopped over at Bridgewater and went to Mrs Briggs for the night.

March 7. Tuesday.

Over to Normal Hall to see Miss Woodward. Had an hour's talk, & then went with her to the school house, and into Mr Martin's Eng. Lit. class. It was like old times to see him again, cool and quiet, now listening attentively to each individual opinion, then asking one of his clear, concise questions that went to the heart of the matter in hand.

Mr Briggs is building a new house, and I went with Mrs B. after dinner to see it. - I had supper with Miss Woodward. It was a select and merry little tea party - Mr & Mrs Boyden, Mrs Goding, and Miss Horne (the elocution teacher) making six in number. In the eve we went into Mrs Boyden's parlor, where the lady-teachers met to read Shakspeare - "Othello" tonight. Last winter they met once a week to discuss art & artists; this term they are studying Shakspeare. Miss Mary Leonard and her sister Edith were present.

March 8. Wednesday.

Over to bid Miss Woodward goodbye; a drive to the station in the rain with kind Mr Briggs; then Boston, 330 Shawmut Ave. & a warm welcome from Frank Tyler.

March 26. Sunday.

My 23d birthday. Mr Holden gave me seven dollars to spend for music. Lizzie Longley is here for a fortnight & we have pleasant times rooming together. Frank made this plan that Lizzie & I might know & like each other.

April 4. Tuesday.

Charles Carleton Coffin and Mrs Sawyer here to tea. The former is plain and rather rugged in appearance (not unlike the Abraham Lincoln type). He gave us a thrilling description of a cavalry charge at the battle of Gettysburg. Mrs Sawyer sung to us. A charming evening.

April 6. Thursday.

Received a letter from Mr Niles (firm of Roberts Brothers - Publishers). He wrote that H.H. had sent him my letter to her to read, that she had sent a set of her books to Relief & he had added a few as his own gift, and the letter concluded with "If you could write the story of Relief Paine with the same sweet naturalness that characterizes your letter to H.H. it would bring you fame and fortune. Cordially yours Thomas Niles." The package of books had been sent to the Cape and with it, two notes to Relief and myself from Mrs Helen Jackson, who also sent me her "Bits of Talk." How happy Relief will be!

April 7. Friday.

Emily went with me to call on Mr Niles this morning. He had not come in, so we waited in his little office, which was filled with papers, books and pictures of authors. I noticed a framed letter from Miss Alcott thanking him for a Christmas gift of money and for "the kindness that had made the thorny up hill path of a writer blossom with such beautiful little surprises." Mr Niles came, tall, dark eyed, gray hair & mustache, rather stern looking until he smiled. I tried to thank him for Relief and myself, and he gave me advice and encouragement.

April 8. Saturday.

Through the kindness of the Hoveys, Lizzie and I went to see "Paul Revere" at the Museum.

April 9. Sunday.

Went with Nettie & Lizzie Longley to hear the great Easter oratorio "Bach's Passion Music" at Music Hall.

April 10. Monday.

Lizzie returned to Northampton.

April 11. Tuesday.

May Greely came over to dine and bid me goodbye. She brought over her M.S. of "Dorothy Dudley" that I might look it over and give my opinion on Major Heath's love making.

April 14. Friday.

Went to Lucy Taylor's for the last few days of my stay in Boston. Musicale at aunt Nettie's in the evening. Harry Cornell & wife, Mr Chenery, Mrs Delano, Mrs Bryant, the Badgers, Greenleafs, Lords, Addie & Priscie Nickerson, Mr & Mrs Robins, Lucy & myself. I enjoyed it, Mr Chenery's singing best of all.

April 16. Sunday.

Easter. To Mr Hale's church in A.M. Mrs West sung "I know that my Redeemer liveth." In the evening, Lyman & Eugene came in for a sing.

April 19. Wednesday.

Went to bid Frank Tyler & aunt Olivia goodbye. Frank said, "I wish you had just come, and I never said anything more honestly in my life. Goodbye and God bless you, my Carl [sic]." I left there with muff and hat box, met aunt Dede who bestowed upon me a package of Boston chip, and I entered a market and bought two bunches of radishes, as my last chance for the season of eating my favorites. We never see any at the Cape, & I think the folks will be glad of them.

April 20. Thursday.

Left Boston in 8 A.M. train and at the first glimpse of blue water & whiff of salt air, knew how homesick I was. My sea, and the white gleam of the cliffs over the water, and the delicious breeze so salt and strong! How I love it all! Then home and its dear people. I was unpacked & settled before nightfall, for of course mother could not rest until I had emptied my trunk! aunt Olive & Bell called.

April 24. Monday.

Oh, the sly little puss! Here is May Greely engaged!! Think of her art-less innocence in coming to me for advice on the art of love making! "He" is Mr William Goodridge of Cambridge. Frank Tyler wrote me this today.

April 27. Thursday.

Went to Relief's and carried her lovely surprise, my first chance since coming home. I made her guess before telling her, but she could think of nothing unless I had found my "artist" who could paint a picture of Relief for me. When she knew, I doubt if there was a happier heart under the sun this afternoon. The books were given her & described, one by one, and after she grew weary with holding them all, she chose two to keep beside her - H.H.'s "Verses," and a little book of Christina Rossetti's sent by Mr Niles. On these her hand rested, often passing lovingly over the fresh pages and binding to learn them by heart, and only leaving them to carry H.H.'s little note to her lips or to her cheek caressingly, and to seek my hand with a mute "thank you." I wish H.H. could see her! Mr Niles has sent her five books - Jean Ingelow's "Poems," Mr Hale's "In His Name" and "Ten Times One is Ten," "Quiet Hours" (compiler unknown) and "Annus Domini" by Christina Rossetti.

Relief told me about her early life today, when she and Asenath were children. The two little sisters (Relief the elder by two years) were insep-arable, playing happily together, and taking the long walk to school every day, carrying their dinner. It used to shock and grieve them to see the angry wrangling of other sisters; it was strange and hard to understand. They never had anything approaching to a quarrel, save once, when they differed about some little thing, and Asenath caught up a plaything, (half in fun, half in a pet) and threw it at Relief. It did not hurt the child, but it was hours before she recovered from the hurt of seeing Sene do such a thing, and Asenath cried as heartily as Relief. At school, Relief was shy and reserved, shrinking from any rough play, and devoted to her books.

April 28. Friday.

Thomas Sears came in this morning of an errand, and as he turned to go, looked back at me and said laughingly, "You don't ask if Relief slept any last night! We thought she would need watchers, she was so excited and happy over her books. It is wonderful how much books are to her." His face was bright with pleasure, and I thought "How beautiful it is that Relief's gladness makes you all so glad!"

May 1. Monday.

Wrote to H.H. and to Mr Niles, giving Relief's messages and my own thanks.

May 4. Thursday.

The Shakspeare Club met here in eve to read "Coriolanus."

May 10. Wednesday.

The third day of rain. Such greenness and fragrance out of doors. Steenie came from school bringing me a lovely handful of white anemones and some purple meadow violets. Peach blossoms are rosy in the garden, and the west bank is sprinkled thick with blue peri-winkle or myrtle that spreads every year.

May 11. Thursday.

Last meeting of the season, at Emily Lincoln's, of the Shakspeare Club. Review of the winter's work by Mr Coffin; Mr Dawes read Sprague's "Ode on Shakspeare"; Ida Winslow, a poem; and I, H.H's "Choice of Colors" from "Bits of Talk." Mr Coffin, Ida & I were appointed committee of entertainment for our next meeting, in December or January.

May 13. Saturday.

Steenie brought me mayflowers from the bank by our pond, large sweet clusters, very pink, - such beauties!

I witnessed a curious May mood this afternoon. Standing in the library doorway, looking out at the sunny loveliness of the day, suddenly came a dash of water drops in my face, and I was looking at the landscape through a glittering mist of rain! Undine at her pranks! The sunlight was not dimmed for a moment, and we had a rainbow whose perfect arch spanned the sky. - In the midst of the sun shower, a small funeral procession went by. I learned that Mr Stacy was dead, & heard his story. He was the father of the three little children who died of diptheria last Fall in the eastern part of the town. He moved to Yarmouth at once and has been struggling along through the winter poor, hungry, out of work. They say he died of a broken heart. He came of a respectable family in Bridgewater, married a girl whose relatives were rough, depraved people, from whom he took her at once and came to Brewster, where they lived a hand-to-mouth existence in a small house by the sea, but the children made that hard life happy. Then all died but the baby, and the wife wanted to go home to her mother in Yarmouth. So he went, to the people from whom he had been glad to escape, and there he died. If poverty and disappointment and sorrow can break a human heart, then his was surely broken.

May 18. Thursday.

I went to the pond this morning, and found anemones & mayflowers, yellow cinquefoil, violets, purple & white, strawberry blossoms, and young ferns, some not yet unrolled from their compact little balls. In the garden I found periwinkle, fragrant yellow jonquils, peach and cherry blossoms. These, with scarlet geraniums, were for Relief's may basket, which I carried to her this afternoon. She was so pleased with the flowers and gifts. I read in "Idylls of the King," and we talked. She says such pretty things about Asenath's baby, who is a rosy, lovely little child. Today it was, – "I used to call baby my snowdrop, but she is my little rainbow now, because she looks through smiles and tears, and is a bright, dancing, changeable little thing, - from one mood to another. She has a large share of my heart and I tell Sene she is half mine."

Little Maggie Murphy went home tonight. She has been spending a few days with Bessie. I miss the quiet little figure in the blue dress, the great dark eyes that followed us about, and the sound of those active little crutches on the floor. She is but seven years old, and is the quietest of the quiet. Half the time you would not notice her presence in the room, save for the shining of her eyes. She had never seen a piano, and said softly, "Oh! what a high table!" After that, whenever I touched the keys, I would shortly find little Maggie on a low stool beside me, with her eyes on my face. She repeated some verses with evident appreciation of their meaning, and talked intelligently about birds and their habits. She liked to follow aunt Mary & myself when we worked in the garden, and she would play croquet with Steenie in spite of crutches, deftly carrying the mallet under her arm. There was always a smile on her face, and her cheery patience was touching to see. She has suffered for a year with hip disease, brought on by a fall at school, and now she must use crutches for a year at least, and one poor little foot is several inches from the floor. It is hard to see a little child suffer.

May 19. Friday.

The Roland Crosbys have purchased a lot in our cemetery, and are moving the bodies of their dead from their East Brewster lot. Today, the body of Sally Crosby, a young girl who died twenty-two years ago, was found to look as fresh and unchanged as on the day she was buried. The hair was smooth & bright, the face unaltered, the dress perfectly preserved, and her mother came and looked upon her after all these years! She died in Chicago, and was placed in an airtight metallic coffin, the maker saying that her body would be preserved for some years, but he could not tell how many.

May 21. Sunday.

Capt. Elisha Bangs resigned his superintendency of the Sunday School.

May 26. Friday.

The pink flowering almond is in bloom, and lilies of the valley are hiding behind their broad green leaves. I sent some to Relief, by aunt Mame, this afternoon.

May 27. Saturday.

The horse chestnuts are magnificent, their great green cones all alight with the smaller flower cones, like a glory of Chinese lanterns at a festival. Scargo Hill is softly blue in the distance and gives me pleasure.

May 28. Sunday.

Such a "field of the cloth of gold" I saw on my way to church. Thousands of buttercups holding up their exquisite bright cups to the sun. The dandelions lose in comparison, but they have grown rank and tall now, and their gold is turning to silver, and taking to itself wings, flies away. The silver abeles are at their loveliest, – as if wonderful cloud mists had drifted too near the earth, and been caught in their branches. Steenie & I walked to the cemetery at sunset. It was quiet and beautiful, full of whispering trees and the goodnight twitter of birds. I brought back larch tassels, and the young red of birch leaves.

June 7. Wednesday.

Unitarian Conference at Nantucket. About twenty went from Brewster, among them Hattie Burrill, mother and myself. We went by rail to Hyannis, and there took the steamer for the island. It was a lovely day, and we had a pleasant passage in the River Queen – formerly a dispatch steamer on the Potomac river, belonging to President Lincoln. His state room is kept exactly as he left it. Mrs Winslow and Mrs Pineo had the use of it today.

I sat in the stern of the steamer enjoying the blue sparkling water, the shadowy sails in the distance, and just before reaching the island, the dark clouds in the southwest that rolled up to the zenith, showing that somewhere were rain & thunder. Entering Nantucket harbor, the channel wound in zig-zag fashion between stakes & buoys set to mark the dangerous shoal places. Nantucket looks like a small city, with its wharves & shipping, its roofs and spires. We rounded the long, low, sandy point with its red light house that marks one side of the harbor, & made fast to the wharf which was black with people and waiting carriages. No wonder that Drake thought the wharf "would be the best place in which to take the census of Nantucket." We waited on the steamer to be assigned to the various stopping places. Mr Dawes appeared with his list, and said mother and I were to go to Mrs Perry's, but Hattie B. stepped forward with an imploring "Pray don't leave me out," and Mr Dawes looked puzzled, so I gave up my place to Hattie, – whereupon he proposed that I go with him to Mrs Starbuck's. While this was being discussed, young Mr Starbuck came forward, was introduced, and carried me off through the steamer and across the wharf to his carriage, and we drove to Matthew Starbuck's on Main street. Mrs Starbuck, a fine-looking lady with gray hair, welcomed me at the door. After going to my room, I came downstairs & met Mr E. N. Winslow (C.C.R.R. Superintendent) & wife, and Mrs Peirson a Nantucket lady who had come in to tea, probably to see Mr Dawes. He was once the pastor here, and Mrs Starbuck is apparently greatly attached to him. No wonder! In a few moments, Mr Dawes came in, the folding doors were thrown open, disclosing the dining room, and we had supper. After that, we went out behind the house to see Mrs Starbuck's ferneries, wonderful lilies of the valley, the fine English ivy that covers nearly one side of the great brick house, and the cro-quet ground where is room enough for several matches to be played at a time. Mr Starbuck has just planted a maple for centennial tree. He escorted me to church in the evening, where we heard a sermon from Mr Cudworth.

74

June 8. Thursday.

Another fine day, sunny and cool. After breakfast, Mr Starbuck went with me to call on mother & Hattie, who were not far from us, at a Mrs Perry's, in a real old Nantucket house, with railed platform on the roof, built for a convenient outlook in the old whaling times. These breezy lookout places abound, & are one of the features of Nantucket. - Mrs Edward Perry is cordial, pleasant & hospitable. We walked to church at 9.30, where Mr Starbuck left me, saying he should return & escort me to the collation. Chancel and pulpit were bright with flowers, mostly wild flowers, so rich in coloring and so tastefully arranged, that the effect was really beautiful. We sat until nearly 2 P.M. listening to Colonel Needham's essay and the animated discussion to which it gave rise. Then we adjourned till 6.30 P.M. for an afternoon of rest & recreation. We went first to the hotel near by and partook of the cold collation provided for all, and then Mr Starbuck walked home with me, his carriage was brought round, and we drove 7 ½ miles to Siasconset. The road lies over lonely prairie land, but I found the wide levels beautiful with soft shades of brown and yellow & numerous patches of wild flowers. Wintergreen is abundant, and in its season, the Nantucket boys may gather quarts of the spicy red berries. Another berry found here is known as "mealy plum," Mr Starbuck said. Buttercups waved in the sunlight like troops of yellow butterflies, white innocence bloomed fair and free, and all the way, in such lavish abundance that they sprung from the very sand, grew the Nantucket violets, deep purple flowers with hearts of gold. Earlier in the season, the little field violets flourish, but with June comes this larger, richer growth, intense in color. I thought them garden folk when I first saw them in Mrs Starbuck's parlor.

Siasconset or S'conset as it is clipped by the islanders, was originally but a rough fishing hamlet. The narrow streets of one story houses, with their miniature front yards are unaltered, but S'conset is gradually becoming a place of summer resort, many of the townspeople have built cottages here for summer residence, picnics, &c. and several hotels have been erected. Many of the fishermen move to town in summer and rent their S'conset homes to summer visitors.

We met mother and Hattie here with Mrs Perry and they visited with us Mr Starbuck's cottage to which he had brought the key. After they left, I took a walk with my cicerone along the bluff that overlooks the sea, and the beach where small fish houses were clustered, and a long row of dories lay upon the sand just above high water mark. We went through queer bits of streets, odoriferous of fish, by little yards gay with flower beds or filled with fish flakes. In one was the highly-colored figure of a woman carved from wood for the figure head of a ship, and against some of the houses hung a motley collection of smaller figure heads. We visited the pump in the centre of the village for a draught of S'conset water, and came back to the cottage for a lunch before driving home. Mr Starbuck had a story to tell, often most amusing, of every house we passed. We reached home too late for church, had supper by ourselves, as the others had gone out to tea, rested & chatted for an hour, then strolled over to the church in time for the finish of the sermon, and to the reception at Mrs Sanford's.

I heard something of the Starbuck family history today. This red brick mansion is the central one of three, all built by the grandfather of my new acquaintance Bradley Starbuck, who gave one to each of his sons.

Matthew Starbuck, Bradley's father, was an eccentric and dissipated man who died last winter. His eldest daughter, Caroline, (a fine looking woman, if her picture tells the truth), married in opposition to his wishes, and he never saw her or spoke of her again. She lives in California, and is coming on with her children this summer for her first visit home. Two other daughters, married, and a younger son Horace, make up the family.

Bradley, the elder son, is handsome, warm-hearted and generous, evidently a favorite in town, but like the father, has been dissipated, has run through a fortune of $20,000, and in consequence of his wild life, is now living apart from his wife and child - a boy of six who is very dear to him. Since his father's death, he has been with his mother on the Island, away from city temptations, and is trying to lead a sober & steady life. His wife is in New York with her friends, and rumor says will never return to him. His mother is one of those rare characters who bear the heaviest trials, bravely and cheerfully, and who keep on loving and forbearing through everything. Now that his father's influence is removed, and he is with his mother, there seems some hope for Bradley Starbuck's future. He seems one who might be easily influenced for either good or evil; rather weak in will, yet still a lovable character. I found him most courteous and gentlemanly - a pleasant companion. He is a good sailor and sportsman, fond of a horse and a gun. He showed me the latter with pride, and I liked the way in which his strong brown hands handled the reins over his spirited chestnut Orion. He reminded me a little of George Bangs.

I have found it good fun to be "a delegate." It is something to have eaten bluefish and been the guest of a Starbuck on Nantucket Island, and to have gathered the Nantucket violets on their native heath. I enjoyed the Conference speakers also, tho' I rather think I have Mr Starbuck to thank for the cream of my good time! I was struck by a remark Mrs Starbuck made tonight with much earnestness – "We make a great mistake in life by so often gathering thorns when we might gather roses, - in really <u>choosing</u> the thorns."

June 9. Friday.

A fair day, with fresh breeze. I was downstairs before 6 A.M. to go with Mr Dawes, (and Ida Winslow & Emily Lincoln who are staying opposite at the Barneys) to visit the Unitarian church tower on Orange St. We climbed the dusty, winding stair, & looked off over the quiet streets and railed roofs of Nantucket to the wharves & waiting steamers, the sandy point with its red light house, and the blue, glittering sea beyond; finding all beautiful in the fresh morning light. I was interested in the great bell, & learned that it was brought from Lisbon by one of the Nantucket captains for his church. It bears a Portuguese inscription as follows:

"As bom Jesus do Monte completao seus votos: os devotos de Lisboa, offerecendo lke hum completao Jogo de seis sinos para chamar os povos: adoralo no seu Sanctuario.

Jose Domingues Dacosta ofez em Lisboa no anno 1810."

which translated is

"To the good Jesus of the Mount
The Devotees of Lisbon in fulfillment of their vows, offer to Him this one (i.e. Bell) to complete a chime of six bells to call the people to adore him in his Sanctuary.

Jose Dominguez De Costa made it in Lisbon, A.D. 1810."

A night watchman is posted in this tower, to keep a look out for fires (this has been the custom since the great fire of 1846), a tell tale mark that must be moved every fifteen minutes, bearing witness to the faithfulness of his watch & ward. The town crier old Billy Clark, who says that he himself is "the only live man in Nantucket," is a character. He makes of this church tower a daily observatory, that he may announce the arriving & departing steamers. He passed the house last eve, ringing a large dinner bell with deafening emphasis, to call attention to his stentorian announcement that the steamer would sail at 8 A.M. His wits are not of the clearest, and during the war, he was often primed with nonsense speeches by the mischief-loving boys, at one time convulsing Nantucket with the lusty declarations "The Rappahannock has crossed the Potomac!" He has grown more wary, if not wiser, of late years. Mr Dawes found him at his post of observation on the roof of the tower, this morning. Returning, we passed the work room of a Mr Folger, and Mr Dawes took us in to see a "nest" of baskets, nine of them, one within another, the largest a bushel measure, handsomely woven, strong and close. After breakfast, Mr Starbuck drove us to the steamer, & escorted me to the deck where I found mother and Hattie. I enjoyed our sail back, tho' the rough and tumble sea made half the passengers quite miserable with seasickness; but I loved the bounding, rocking motion, the white-crested waves and strong wind, and wished the voyage were longer.

June 30. Friday.

Goodbye to June. Here is the floral list for the month: – buttercups, clover, wild geranium, flower de luce, swamp honeysuckle, field daisies, pale pink arethusa growing in lovely patches by the pond, wild roses, grass pinks, cranberry blossoms - little tongues of red & yellow flame, red laurel, water lilies, yellow loosestrife, elder, red lilies.

In the garden - roses of all kinds, syringa, honeysuckle, money wort, larkspur, sweet peas, monkshood pansies.

July 16. Sunday.

Yesterday a Union picnic was held at Oak Bluffs, Martha's Vineyard. Steenie went, and has been giving me an account of his day's experience. He told a capital story of all his doings from leaving home in the early morning to his return at night. As usual, nothing had escaped his notice & activity. He visited cottages, and talked with Irish women and children, rowed on a lake, ate icecream (sic) at a restaurant, rode in the horse-cars, visited an Indian camp, explored the steamers, questioned the men and risked his neck leaping ashore from a steamer just moving off, marched with the procession, lost his lunch basket (of course not until after he had eaten the lunch), picked up the usual amount of old acquaintances in the crowd, and never thought of being tired till he reached home and was glad to drop asleep at once. He told it all in boy fashion. The view as they steamed across the Sound and looked off at the cottage city & camp ground, he said was "Splendid! all covered with birch and maple trees, so many of them that you couldn't get out of the shade!" One incident was quite amusing. Steenie, Austin Keith and Wallace Foster wandered off together for a walk, and came across a pretty child of three or four years, playing near a cottage, with whom they talked. They were in doubt whether it was a boy or girl, until the little fellow began to climb a tree, when Wallace gave a sigh of relief and said "It's a boy, after all!" They wanted a drink of water, and the child went to get it. He returned, the pretty boy, his yellow curls shining in the sun, but with one very grimy little hand on the inside of the cup for more secure holding. The boys looked at each other, and Wallace said, "Well, where's your pump? I guess we shall want some more," so the child trotted off again, Steenie & Wallace following. They rinsed the glass thoroughly, had their drink, and were half way back, when Austin called out "Bring me some." They kept on, & after them came the patient little fellow, innocently ready, carrying the glass, with one brown little paw half immersed in water. There was a great laugh at Austin's expense and the child was made happy with a five cent piece.

July 27. Thursday.

Addie, Priscie and Mrs Myra Nickerson called on us in "The Castle" this eve.

July 31. Monday.

The July flowers were yellow loosestrife, clethra, wild indigo with yellow flowers and dark blue seed pods, jewel weed, purple thoroughwort, pink Rutland Beauty or wild morning glory, – all these found in & near the swamps. Sweet old maids' pinks camp out in our orchard, and in the garden a great trumpet vine swings itself in & out of a young elm, bearing tight sealed buds and flaming blossoms.

In gardens also, bloom coreopsis red & yellow, great sunflowers, nasturtiums, moneywort, balsams, white & red, smoke, mignonette, and sweet peas in every shade of white, pink & purple.

Toward the end of the month, frogs and crickets sing o' nights.

August 16. Wednesday.

Our Fair opened this eve in Knowles's hall. Mrs D. Bangs has made a bower of the refreshment table. All the tables are pretty & tasteful, but ours really takes the lead. It is most abundantly supplied with pretty articles and so far we have taken the most money. Little Emmie occupied a red and white booth between the doors, where she guarded her grab box, and was an active & attractive little sales woman. She had also a toy cart filled with buttonhole bouquets and drawn by a spirited wooden steed in cherry ribbon harness.

August 18. Friday.

I took noon train to Barnstable. Annie met me at the station. Mrs Handy, Ella, Leon, Jamie & Mamie at home. Edward came in the evening train. Lucy Thayer, a pretty cousin from the West, came to tea. Crambo & Criticism & Magnetism in the eve.

August 19. Saturday.

Croquet in the morning. Annie & I visited the barn & had a good talk. The wind sweeps through open opposite doors, & there is a lovely view of the water. Here is a hammock and a wide old sofa, & many pleasant hours of family reading & sewing are spent in this place. In P.M. we drove to the Yarmouth camp ground, returning in evening train.

August 20. Sunday.

We had an old-fashioned "sing," after breakfast to please uncle Isaac who lives next door. Campmeeting again in afternoon. A sudden shower descended in the midst of the service and drove all to the shelter of tents & cottages. The evening service was one to be remembered. The swinging lantern lights on the trees shone on the listening faces of the people, showed the white gleam of tents in the distance and the moving shadows of onlookers, and silvered the lower tree branches, while the masses of foliage above were in deep shadow; the wind went sounding through the grove until the trees swayed & quivered and the canvas stretched above the speakers' stand bellied and tugged like a sail at sea; and clear through the singing, speaking and rushing wind, we heard the katy dids calling. We were quite chilled on the cold return drive, but after lunch in the warm dining room, we sat around the fire giving Mrs Handy the story of our experiences which she enjoyed in her quiet, hearty fashion. Ella is the fun maker and kept us laughing. The Handys always give their mother this after share in the fun.

August 21. Monday.

Ed went in early train. I went in next door to sing to the family's aunt Hannah, who is an invalid. She leaned back against the pillows in her easy chair, pale & feeble, but her face brightened as she listened. "It must give yourself & others so much pleasure to be always able to sing like that," she said.

Home again in P.M. Steenie met me with an eager "Hullo, sister! I've missed you like fury." I went to work folding clothes, a pretty house hold task.

August 27. Sunday.

A run in the fields at sunset. Wonderful color in the western sky, the clouds in north like a range of mountains. Found cardinal flowers by the pond, like spikes of fire, and blackberries were sweet & plenty.

August 29. Tuesday.

Drove to Cliff Pond at sunset with Nettie and Emily. Oh, the lovely shadowy water and wooded cliffs! the stillness broken only by the sweet singing of a single bird. I sprang from the carriage & ran along the sandy beach, finding flowers – five varieties, the golden rod the most beautiful.

August 31. Thursday.

An afternoon with Relief. She had ready for me a quantity of marsh rosemary, blue and fresh.

The first of August, slender spires of golden rod appear and the first white asters; at its close they are in full glory. Pink spirea, purple milkweed, butter & eggs, heavy golden tansy, cardinal flowers, pink hibiscus, feathery reed grass & darker foxtail grasses are August children. In the garden grow thyme, nasturtiums, sweet peas, double scarlet geranium, garden asters of purple, red & white, sweet alyssum, mignonette, and four o'clocks.

September 1. Friday.

A family picnic in the grove by the sea, Walter's little yacht dancing attendance on the blue water.

September 4. Monday.

Aunt Nettie, Walter & I en route for Philadelphia. Waited at Middleboro nearly an hour. Saw Fall River & its great, flat-roofed mills, with the red sunset light on its river, - & so on board the steamer. Another delay of an hour & a half, waiting for Boston trains, but at last we were off. Seventeen hundred persons on board, no stateroom to be had, & we must mount guard over the drawing room chairs to secure even that resting place for the night. It rained, but I sought the deck occasionally in spite of this, to look out on the misty water & watch the steady progress of the boat. Young Fred Nickerson & wife were on board. Also Mrs Julia Ward Howe. We stopped at Newport. I went outside, but beyond a confused vision of moving lights, wet wharves, the strain & creak of ropes, the rush of passengers over the gangway, saw nothing of the place. Soon after 10 P.M. the band stopped playing & people tried to compose themselves to sleep. It was an amusing sight, worth for once the loss of a night's rest. Each chair had its occupant, and the floor was laid thick with mattrasses [sic]. Here lay two men, arm in arm, like comrades resolved to bear the worst together; there, one unfortunate, with a chair for his head & one for his feet, nothing between, struggled to maintain a horizontal position; two men lay, head to head, at Nettie's feet, and just beyond, a young woman was quietly sleeping, her face hidden by her falling hair; one proper maiden lady waited till all was quiet, then rose to a sitting posture & proceeded to crimp her hair. The man in chair next mine was in a strong draught and tied a white handkerchief about his baldness & thin scattering locks, a corner of which waved wildly in the breeze. "Press where you see my white plume shine!" I whispered to Walter. My neighbor suddenly clapped on a beaver over the handkerchief with such absurd effect that I shook with suppressed laughter, until I found him peering round the corner with timid anxiety, evidently thinking me a dangerous neighbor, possibly subject to fits. We heard swearing & snoring and joking & grumbling, but mostly laughing, for good humor prevailed. Walter & I laughed over the queer sights until one o'clock, & then had snatches of sleep until morning.

September 5. Tuesday.

We were glad to stretch our cramped selves at dawn & go on deck for fresh air and the sunrise. It was beautiful – the first flushes of rosy light, the clear gold stealing after to spread up & over the sky, the slow coming up from the sea of the great sun itself, the water flashing into quick light & sparkle, the silver froth & mist of our wake, the exquisite blue of the morning sky. The sail up New York harbor is wonderful. We looked on green shores, with forts & long lines of buildings, boats & vessels of all sizes & kinds, steamers gay with people & music, & on the solid stone towers that stand one on either side the river, with four slender lines uniting them, nucleus of the new bridge. New York at last – a quick walk through the Fulton Market, past white aproned market women & tempting piles of summer fruit & vegetables, to the Cortlandt ferry; over the river to Jersey city; dinner - most needful & welcome; and the train for Philadelphia. We dashed across green New Jersey, almost too tired & sleepy to admire, but I do remember seeing a canal boat in lazy motion, & the silver sheen of buckwheat in blossom; the red & yellow wealth of the fruit orchards, the deep red of the soil (is that the secret of the rich coloring of its fruit?) and the beauty of quiet shaded streams. I thought of Washington & his Christmas experience as I crossed the Delaware. – Our train entered the station just outside the Exposition grounds and it was like coming into a city. We were glad to escape from the noise & confusion in an omnibus, & drove off to the Grand Exposition hotel. We slept soundly all night, tho' on harder beds than we had ever imagined.

September 6. Wednesday.

At 9 A.M. we entered the grounds & took the train on the narrow gauge road for a general view of the buildings. It was thrilling – that first sight of the crowds of people, the great buildings crowned with flags of all nations, our own banner high above all, the lesser buildings – Swedish, Turkish, Japanese, Moorish, German, Canadian, &c. the broad walks, rich grass plots, & beds of blooming flowers. We then entered Machinery Hall. It is indescribable – the whir & rush & ceaseless motion of those miles of machinery! The great machines with their belts & shafts & pistons seemed like Titans at work. I enjoyed watching the carpet loom – the swift shuttles flying back & forth, the darting out of the long steel rule, or bar that pushed each thread to place, the bright-fabric slowly rolling over toward me, - such beautiful order & steady growth! If the machines are Titans, what can be said of their Master – the great Corliss engine the regular throb of whose iron heart sets the pulse beating in all the belt & shaft machinery in the great building. Its huge boilers are outside the Hall in a building devoted especially to them. The engine stands on a circular platform in the centre of the Hall, & is always surrounded by a crowd. I was there at the noon hour when it stopped work for a season & almost instantly the machinery all over the building was stilled. A curious effect!

Words fail me to describe the giant locomotives; the light Canadian canoes and paddles; the tempting candies & the candy making; the great water tank & the silvery jets that crossed & re-crossed above it, thrown by force of steam pumps; the steamer models; the famous life raft; the beautiful ice yacht so alive that it seemed held in leash & impatient to dart away out of sight; the Brazilian field guns & swords and uniforms. We saw Mr Voorhees for a moment & appointed a meeting at 5 o'clock. Then we left Machinery Hall as its mid day chimes were playing, & the rest of the day was spent in the Main Building.

The beauty of color, shape, life, motion and distance in that Main Building, flashed upon us in one dazzling whole, as we looked far up the shining vista and realized that what seemed to us the end was only the centre of the edifice. I caught my breath & turned for relief into one of the nearest departments which proved to be Jamaica. I lingered to see the coffee, nutmegs, sugar, pomegranates, great slabs of pure white wax; the hats, scarfs, fans &c. made from the coarse, yellowish-white lace bark; and the fine woods, cedar & mahogany, & lignum vitae with its dark-veined centre. There were great sections of trees, the rough bark outside, the inside polished to show the rich grain of the wood. – We passed next to Canadian fireplaces, furs, skates, moccasins & snow-shoes. – A step from these & we were in India. I admired the carved black wood furniture from Bombay; the cocoons, silkworms & heavy skeins of raw silk yellow & white; laughed at a rude native plough; and could see no beauty, although I tried, in a cashmere carpet that was probably worth thousands.

I was rather disappointed in Italy, did not like the bronzes or the jewelry. There were some fine corals from Naples, however. I was looking at a heavy necklace of gold & sapphires, marked "Sold to the Empress of Brazil," when a brisk, dark-eyed little woman stepped up to me and said, "Can you show me a diamond necklace, please?" I looked, but found none made entirely of diamonds. "Then will you be so kind as to show me a diamond in any shape?" she asked. "I have never seen a diamond." I pointed out a sparkling arrow made of diamonds alone, and her black eyes viewed it with eager interest.

I liked best the photograps on the walls of this Italian court, the beautiful work in carved & inlaid woods – bedsteads, frames, tables, cabinets, &c. and a simple little fountain, a stone foundation green with creeping vines, that upheld two children under an umbrella.

The water spouted from the umbrella tip, flowed over its surface & splashed at the little feet, keeping the vines fresh & bright. The boy held the umbrella over the little girl's head with great care. There were few people that did not pause to smile at the merry child faces under the umbrella.

The iron masters of <u>Sweden</u> have a fine exhibit of their native iron & steel, and you are much impressed by the industry & intelligence of her people. The military display is good. There are fine bits of delicate porcelain, & many rich furs. I saw an eider duck robe of soft brown and gray and white, & a martin geyst cloak of rich yellow & brown. The life like groups of costumed peasants attract crowds. One group consisted of a poor peasant mother bowed in deep grief over the cradle of her dead baby and holding its little waxen hand, while on the floor beside her a small black coffin waited for its burden. With book in hand, grave & sympathizing, the priest looked down upon her, and beyond, sat the father who had drawn the grieving little sister of the dead child to his side. - A happier group showed an old clockmaker seated at work. His wife, with her hand on his shoulder, pleaded for a favorable answer to a stalwart young fellow holding the hand of their rosy cheeked daughter.- Still another was a Lapp in his sledge, checking the speed of his reindeer, to talk with a fur clad woman with a baby slung to her neck, who stood on the frozen snow. – <u>Norway's</u> iron exhibit takes the form of an ancient Scandinavian war vessel with dragon-shaped prow, & an armed warrior on deck like a veritable Viking. Here, too, we saw the long and narrow Norwegian sledges, & a wealth of furs, magnificent lynx, wolf & bear skins dressed with claws, head &c. complete even to the small black twinkling eyes and red tongue hanging out of the mouth, & so lifelike that you would not have been surprised had the savage growl also been preserved. – <u>Great Britain</u> had a fine display of tile work. I liked also the great crystal chandeliers, the simple beauty of a terra cotta pulpit – red, buff, dark blue, the solid handsome English furniture, the beautiful porcelain, the Scotch jewelry, especially the cairngorms reddish brown, transparent stones, some of them with an amber lustre. – <u>France</u> displays rich silks & laces, and life size figures & groups for church altars - the Nativity, the dead Christ in the arms of his mother, &c. I liked the figure of an angel holding a swinging censer, in robe of delicate yellow, with a glad, childlike face and fair, waving hair. – In <u>Switzerland</u> we found watches & music boxes, of course, and a lovely carved oak chalet with cuckoo clock within, but we had but ten minutes to devote to this section.

Aunt Nettie went home with Mr Voorhees to tea, & Walter & I returned to the hotel. I spent the evening on the balcony in company with a young girl whom I found very attractive. She was only fourteen years of age, but looked seventeen. Tall & slender, with lovely dark eyes, fresh color, an abundance of brown hair, simply braided, caught up & tied with cardinal ribbon. She was glad of a companion and so was I. I did not ask her name, but learned that her home was in Great Barrington, Mass., her father a doctor, & that she had a twin brother, Harry. She is still a school girl, but the town is too quiet to satisfy her eager desire for good times.

"There are almost no boys in town, and if we want a party or picnic or sleighride, why, we girls have to get it up, escort each other, and pay the bills." If she were a boy, she would study to be a doctor, for she had a liking for her father's profession, & had some times assisted him in operations – slight ones. "Why not, as it is?" I asked, but she shook her head, laughingly. She talked on, confidingly, until Nettie & the Voorhees appeared, when our tete-a-tete ended.

September 7. Thursday.

A rainy morning, which we spent in Main building. Visited Africa first, where we saw diamonds & ostrich eggs & feathers, brilliant butterflies & birds with plumage of vivid blue and scarlet. – We were a long time among the Chinese wonders. Such exquisite wood carving as we saw, & the tiny pagodas and Chinese junks, boxes & chessmen of carven ivory were as light & beautiful as frost work. In Spain I was most interested in two handsome Spaniards in tasseled scarlet caps & uniforms, who mounted guard over their rich stuffs, saddles, &c. and talked away to each other in their native language. – In Austria were displayed beautiful meerschaums, fine Hungarian opals & garnets, Bohemian glass ware, & amber, pale yellow, or glistening like wet pebbles. An amber chandelier, showed the two kinds beautifully contrasted.

I was disappointed in Germany, even in the Nuremberg toys & dolls, although they were under the special guardianship of St. Nicholas, who smiled graciously upon them, in robe & white beard, with a sprig of Christmas green in his hand. – In the great centre aisle is the Western Union Telegraph department with myriad fine wires rising to the roof, radiating from this centre to all parts of the country. – In the Main Annex can be seen the carriages of different nations, among them, in striking contrast to modern comfort & elegance, was George Washington's old state coach – huge, lumbering, without steps, yet so high from the ground that even the tall General must have found it difficult to enter, and having green blinds, close drawn, that reminded me of the outside state-rooms of a steamer. This afternoon we gave to Memorial Hall. The pictures I liked best were as follows: In <u>Austria</u>, "Venice paying homage to Caterina Cornaro" by Makart. Such rich dresses and fair proud faces, & the beautiful Caterina bends forward from her throne, with such grace & dignity. – In <u>Germany</u>, I liked two pictures: Reichert's "Blinding of Arthur," and Schrader's "Queen Elizabeth signing the Death-Warrant of Mary, Queen of Scots." The former showed in the deep shadow of the background a grim attendant waiting, his presence revealed by the glow of the cruel iron in his hand, – and clinging to Hubert with all the strength of his childish arms, the young Arthur, his slender form, his fair face, his bright falling hair, his blue eyes, so brave and yet so full of pleading, being even more eloquent & pathetic in their mute entreaty than the words on the boy's lips – "O, save me, Hubert, save me! My eyes are out even with the fierce looks of these bloody men."

In Schrader's picture, Elizabeth is seated by a table on which lies the unsigned warrant, and behind her chair stands Burleigh, gravely waiting. Her attitude expresses indecision, she has turned away from the fatal paper, the pen slips between her fingers, and out of her pale proud, troubled face, her blue eyes look into yours, unseeing, but showing plainly the fierce struggle in that passionate heart under the royal velvet and jewels. She hesitates, but there waits the impassive Burleigh, and in a moment she will grasp the pen, dash off her signature, and rise the haughty and relentless queen of England. You forget for the moment, that all this happened long ago, and hold your breath while the fate of Mary Stuart trembles in the balance. – In <u>France</u>, is a terrible "Rizpah Protecting the Bodies of her Sons from the Birds of Prey," by Becker, a sweet, misty "Morning on the Lagoons of Venice," a "School for Young Satyrs" by Prion, full of lusty life & gladness, and the "Death of Julius Caesar" by Clement. Most surprising of all, were the wonderful Gobelin tapestries, so like paintings as to deceive us.

In <u>Great Britain</u>, was Cope's "Taming of the Shrew," a delicious bit of humor. Katherina at table, her elbows planted on the cleared board, her face resting on her clenched hands - a dark beauty, with black frowning brows, - is lost in her rebellious thoughts. The merry servants behind her are carrying off the much abused and discarded dishes; and

Petruchio, turned away from the table, looks up from his reading to throw a laughing side glance at his shaking "sweet Kate," with a glimmer of white teeth under his curling moustache. "Alice" by Wells, is a child standing in a bed of white lilies, her dress as simply pure as the flowers, and her face like the morning in its fresh, glad beauty. I liked Hunter's "Trawlers Waiting for the Darkness." The boat filled with men, rested in the shadow of the land, while the twilight deepened over the still, clear water. You could see the sunset glow grow fainter and the shadows lengthen. – In the <u>United States</u> department, one first sees the "Battle of Gettysburg" a very large painting by Rothermel, ghastly & terrible. "The Old Stage Coach" by Eastman Johnson brings a smile to every face. The body of an old yellow coach has been taken from the wheels, & set on the ground, and the children have taken possession of it. Inside and out, crowd the rosy faces of merry boys and girls. Never, in its palmiest days, did the old coach carry so many and such happy passengers. Four sturdy boys prance and curvet as the horses, and an important young rogue, mounted on the coach box holds reins and whip. – In Rosenthal's "Elaine" I was somehow disappointed. The maiden was lovely, in robe of misty blue, "in her right hand the lily, in her left the letter," her yellow hair fell softly away from a face fair to look upon (the face of Una Hawthorne it is said), yet she was not the Elaine of the poem –

"- all her bright hair streaming down -
And all the coverlid was cloth of gold
Drawn to her waist, and she herself in white
All but her face, and that clear-featured face
Was lovely, for she did not seem as dead
But fast asleep, and lay as though she smiled."

This evening, at supper, we happened to take seats at a table with my bright acquaintance of the balcony and her mother, and I had a pleasant chat with both.

September 8. Friday.

This morning at breakfast, my girl acquaintance came to me to say goodbye as she was to leave in the noon train. – We took the open cars on the narrow gauge road & left them at Brewer's Hall, the entrance to which was green with hop vines. A rapid walk through the building, past its huge tuns, its machinery, its models of brewery & storage house, and also through the Pomological Annex brought us to Agricultural Hall. We took rolling chairs & saw as much as possible in an hour, - the marvelous woods & grains of the West, & the no less interesting display of the East, where Yankee invention makes good the absence of great natural advantages. Portugal showed cheeses; France, wines & confectionery and preserved fruits & meats; Spain, flax, wines, tobacco & boxes of fine raisins; Russia, shoes and white cones of sugar. There were gold fish, and turtles, & South Sea crabs in great tanks; birds of New England in glass cases; bears, bison, elk; a miniature representation of the Gloucester fisheries; a pavilion of Brazilian cotton so like snow that we looked to see it melt before our eyes; and on his perch beside a soldier in faded army blue, stood old Abe, the famous war eagle of Wisconsin. He "served" through three years of the war, was in 25 battles and never lost a battle! The regiment believed victory certain, with old Abe present. He is now fifteen years old. – The horticultural display was far from being in its glory, but it rested me to walk through Horticultural Hall where was no wearying multiplicity of objects, but only the green of foreign trees and plants with the occasional glimmer of a statue amid the greenery. From the outer promenade, on which the galleries open, can be had a fine view of the river and the entire grounds - a scene full of brilliant color and life. We visited the Swedish school house attracted by its swinging windows & quaint cleanly appearance; & thought little Lars and Hertha must find learning pleasant with such help of books, maps & pictures, & keep comfortably warm by the tall porcelain stove. We also saw the Japanese Bazaar with its strange foreign wares & stranger foreign salesmen. We dined at the La Fayette restaurant, & spent the afternoon in Memorial Hall & the Art Annex. In the latter, I saw Bacon's "Boston Boys & Gen. Gage," a bit of spirited life that tells its own story; Bierstadt's "Mt. Hood, Oregon" showing some of the glory of western scenery; and "A Village in Winter" by Breton - the trees & quaint cottages shrouded & heaped with snow, so that you felt the <u>hush</u> of it. There were pictures and pictures however, that seemed to me unworthy their place in the Exhibition.

September 9. Saturday.

We felt so tired and ill this morning that we decided to take the afternoon train for home, - separating, to meet at the station at one o'clock. I breakfasted at the "La Fayette," and took the cars for the Woman's Pavilion, where I had time for only a hasty survey. Beautiful needlework, tapestry, &c. autumn leaves painted on mica, paintings in oil & water color, statuary, models of Canadian convents, Swedish ornaments made of tiny fish scales, silvery & delicate as filigree. I went into the Colorado & Kansas Building, for sake of H.H. and to see the minerals and Mrs Maxwell's life like deer, bears, foxes & birds, shot & stuffed by herself; peeped into an inviting German kindergarten; and entered the U.S. Government Building. A brilliant, prismatic, revolving light first caught my eye, then snowy slabs of Rutland marble; a wealth of Texas cotton, a great Indian dugout, an Arappaho [sic] tent of buffalo skin, models of school houses, from the rude pioneer beginning to the imposing building of today. – In the Army & Navy department were models of transport steamers and sloops of war, cannon & torpedoes, and outside among beds of fragrant heliotrope & other flowers were monster cannon, army tents, ambulances, quartermaster's wagons, a hospital with neat, gauze-curtained beds, and two rather ghastly figures, with bandaged limbs, for representative occupants. The Civil War is not yet so remote that one can look into an ambulance or hospital ward without a shudder of sorrowful remembrance. – I went for a last look at the Corliss Engine & Machinery Hall, then took a rolling chair in Main for my remaining hour, ascending to the gallery for a view of the whole wonderful vista. Met Nettie & Walter at station at 1 P.M. Tedious waiting a crowd, a rush for the cars, a last glimpse of the flags waving over Main Building, the ride across New Jersey, walk through the New York market, steamer, most welcome supper, music, chat with Judge Marston, state rooms & needed sleep.

September 10. Sunday.

Sunrise & Fall River. We dressed hurriedly aunt Nettie quite weak & faint, & left the boat. Train to Boston where we again separated, N. & W. going to Albert's, & I to Frank Tyler's. I waited on the Common for a car, finding it quiet & pleasant & restful in the fresh, early morning, with the yellow elm leaves drifting down on the deserted malls. Found the Tylers at breakfast, Fannie Barnes and her mother with them. I rested and talked through the day with all the dear people, but toward night, aunt Dede came back from a call at Rutland Square, with the news that Nettie was quite ill and had called in Dr. Swan. So after tea (at which meal Mrs Greeley and Philip were present), she escorted me to the Square, where I found poor Nettie in a high fever, and Walter the picture of gloom and despair. At 10.30 P.M. Albert returned from Wenham, & was somewhat amazed to find his house lighted and so unceremoniously taken possession of, but good & helpful as usual. I had an anxious night, for aunt Nettie seemed really very ill, & Walter said the doctor had feared malarial fever.

September 11. Monday.

Nettie rather better. Dr. Swan came in A.M. Albert telegraphed for Emily to come up in after noon train. After dinner, I went round to Frank
90

Tyler's to say goodbye & collect my belongings. The family were at dinner. I ran up to see Mr Holden, had a few minutes talk with the rest until the hack came, said good bye last of all to aunt Dede, Frank, & warm-hearted little Julie at the door, & was off for the Cape. Found Mrs Seabury on train & had her company. I went to aunt Nettie's house, where aunt Mary is staying pro-tem & where I am to rest for a day or two. Mother, Steenie and Frank K. were over there to welcome me.

September 13. Wednesday.

Relief's thirtieth birthday. Half her life has been spent in that little darkened room.

September 21. Thursday.

A few hours with Relief.

September 28. Thursday.

A day with Relief.

September 29. Friday.

Drove to Dennis with Emily & Emmie, leaving aunt Mame at the Dillingham house to call on the solitary Joshua. He showed her, with evident pride, a poetical epitaph (!) written by his wife on the death of her son, beginning "Here lays," &c. which he had carefully framed. The wayside was gay with asters and goldenrod and plu-my smartweed. Bright sumac lit the dark tangle of roadside thickets and we gathered store of red leaves. We passed the Dennis marshes, whose salt odors were invigorating, and whose golden grasses rippled gently under the light touch of the wind. From the edge of the marsh came the faint tinkle of a cow bell, and we could see the moving red of cattle through the trees. Over opposite, on a low hill, waved the brown grasses and glimmered the slanting headstones of the lonely little grave yard that overlooks the marshes. On gray, damp days, this scene always suggests the marshes & dreary churchyard of "Great Expectations" where Pip and the con-vict met.

John Consodine and cow

October 4. Wednesday.

A walk in Capt. Nickerson's cranberry swamp at sunset, crushing the red tangle of blackberry and cranberry vines under foot. Gathered everlasting, golden rod, primroses, cat o'nine tails, fluffy & gone to seed, late clover, field daisies, and asters white & royally purple.

October 9. Monday.

Went the mill drive with Emily. Such lovely hollows & curves & dimples in the low brown hills, filled with sunshine or soft shadow! The far view up Long pond between the purple and red of the woods was beautiful. The west wind beat the water into sparkles of light, and little fleets of ducks went sailing about, dipping & flapping their wings in the blue, gleaming water as if they were playing at snap dragon. There were fields gray - white with everlasting, whose color, softness & grouping - here, crowded together, the flowers fairly jostling each other, there, straggling by twos and threes, - were wonderfully like a moving, distant flock of sheep. We brought home a huge branching stump to feed our hearth fire which roared & crackled in acknowledgment.

October 10. Tuesday.

Emily & I spent the evening with Lola & Abby Bangs.

October 11. Wednesday.

Aunt Nettie came home from the mountains.

October 12. Thursday.

A morning walk with Hattie B. & Duke in the swamps. All nature was enjoying the mild, sunny day. The yellow birches seemed to tremble with excess of pleasure, and the wild grape flung itself along the roadside, in careless grace & abandon, clasping proud tree & modest bush alike in its embrace and forcing them to join in its mad dance.

October 15. Sunday.

The first snow, enough to frost the brown earth, and ice the autumn air.

October 19. Thursday.

Nettie & little Em went to Boston for the winter. I spent the afternoon with Relief, and <u>walked</u> <u>home</u>, for the first time since hurting my foot a year & eight months ago.

October 20. Friday.

Emily went in noon train. I went gunning with Win this afternoon. We were on the shore at sunset, and witnessed glorious changes of color as the sea gleamed and glowed beneath the shifting clouds. The tide was ebbing, and the sun warmed the brown masses of wet seaweed on the sands at my feet. I held a handful to my face breathing in its saltness. Pools of rosy water gleamed among the rocks, and a lovely flush was on the receding sea. Off to the north, a broad bar of golden light seemed to rest on the water, and above it, dusky purple lightened into apple green, which in turn melted into pale, pure blue. Now & then a gull flashed by, and the complaining cry of hundreds of its companions came to me from off back of the Bar. It was so still that far away sounds could be distinctly heard; the cry of seabirds, the striking (five) of the town clock in Dennis, six miles away, the rattle of wheels, barking of dogs, voices and laughter of children in the village behind us.

October 21. Saturday.

A school of blackfish – two hundred of them – were driven ashore near Orleans last night. Thomas Sears was wakened by the puffing and blowing of the great fish and the shouts of the men who pursued them in dories. The men mostly belonged to vessels lying off Provincetown, and made on an average, $100 each, by their night expedition. They sold fifty of the blackfish to Dennis men, and all day carts have been going back & forth, bearing the unwieldy prizes. The head & blubber of two blackfish is sufficient for a cartload. The fish are clumsy monsters, with black, india, rubber-like skins, flesh red, resembling beef, small eyes and sharp pointed teeth in the lower jaw. If one is wounded in the water, the rest all follow it ashore, whether from motives of affection or cannibalism is not known, but it is supposed the former.

November 1. Wednesday.

All Saints Day. Lowell's lines are true of the saints of today –

> "Such lived not in the past alone,
> But thread today the unheeding street."

Relief Paine is my saint. She could not be more of an angel if she were in heaven.

Today, the Burrills left us, & the sewing circle met here.

November 2. Thursday.

I went to see Relief. Sunny, Indian summer weather. I ran down to the shore by the Paine house for a few minutes of enjoyment of sea & marsh. Crept under a boat that was turned on its side & gave shelter from the wind. At my feet was the wild marsh rosemary all tangled with seaweed. Boats lay about on the sands, and white sails gleamed in the distance. The sea was blue, and the sunshine was golden over all. My gaze came back to the little house on the hill, where for fifteen years, Relief has lived in her darkened room, so near this beauty, yet shut out from it all, and she loved it so!

November 11. Saturday.

Last night, Albert wrote us that the "Agenor" was coming up Boston harbor, and tonight our sailor is with us again. It was his first voyage –to Frisco & home via Queenstown & Belfast.

November 18. Saturday.

This morning, the earth was silvered with frost, and the air had a sparkle of frost in it, also. I enjoyed my morning work, & after it, a walk to the shore with aunt Olive. The wind was fresh, and our boys were off in the whale boat, enjoying the breeze & the waves. The gulls were flying about the Great Bar, & in one of the duck rests on shore, crouched a gunner, waving a pair of gulls' wings for a decoy. – Theo & Win walked with me to the Library this P.M. The brothers are quite unlike. Win is sweet-tempered & obliging, easy & self-possessed, with much quiet dignity. The "yellow-haired laddie" has cut close his curly mane. He is a great, strong, broad shouldered fellow who smokes incessantly, sings sea chanties, and speaks the blunt truth at all times. John Fitz, second mate of the Agenor, says that Theo is a good sailor, manly & fearless, quick to learn, & probably in another year will be able for a second mate's position. Theo says he doesn't like a sea life, but I think he does take a rough satis-faction in its danger & hardship. He is glad to be at home – that is evident. He rather glories in his strength, seizes me and carries me about the house, usually ending by putting me on some high place from which I cannot get down without help. He is laying in a stock of picture papers (Frank Leslie's Boys & Girls Weekly) to take to sea, & I tease him by laughing at the sensational pictures & stories (calling them "The brave boy with the bullet," &c.), while he retorts There's a great sight more truth in 'em than in Shakspeare." I shall give him "The Gayworthys" for Christmas gift, & hope he will like Ned Blackmere.

November 22. Wednesday.

I have been lying on the sofa in the twilight, watching the firelight dance and flicker about the room, & its unreal counterpart burning eerily under the silver abeles outside.

> "Under the tree, under the tree,
> When fire out doors burns merrily,
> There the witches are making tea."

Theo has been sitting beside me on the floor in one of his rarely quiet moods, telling about the green Irish shores, and promising me a cairngorm ring when next he comes home.

November 29. Wednesday.

Such a sunrise! How I pity city dwellers, who see the sky only between brick walls! As the sun rose, great masses of golden brown cloud rolled from before it to the zenith & circled the horizon, until reaching the sun again, they veiled its brightness. Then the great cloud circle changed to dusky purple, & rosy cloudlets floated on the outskirts; and finally it all broke up into snowy cloud heaps that drifted slowly through the blue deeps of air. It suggested certain lines in Hiawatha, when

> "Gitche Manito, the mighty,
> Smoked the calumet, the Peace Pipe,
> As a signal to the nations," [sic]
> for this wonderful cloud smoke was
> Ever rising, rising, rising,
> Till it touched the top of heaven,
> Till it broke against the heaven,
> And rolled outward all around it."

November 30. Thursday.

Thanksgiving day. All three of the boys at home, and Walter with us, also. Aunt Olive & Mr Winslow here.

December 9. Saturday.

Cold, cold, cold, with a wild & furious wind. Uncle Isaac Snow is dead, & the remains came down tonight, attended by the Dinsmores, so we have a houseful – Nettie, Mrs Cummings, Mr Dinsmore, Willy and Clarence. They had a cold, uncomfortable drive from the station & were glad enough of the blazing wood fire & a hot supper.

December 10. Sunday.

Funeral in place of the morning service. A profusion of beautiful flowers, (of which we had a generous share, later), spicy pinks, tea roses, bouvardia, & yards upon yards of green smilax. A bright day, but bitter cold. In the evening we sat around the open fire, & Clarence Dinsmore told us of his Siberian adventures.

December 11. Monday.

I went to Boston this noon with the return party. A cold, tiresome train ride, though I enjoyed talking with Mr Dinsmore who told me about hospitals & Parrott guns, carpet looms & pin factories, engines & coins & precious stones. He described his visit to one of the army hospitals during the Rebellion, and the wonderful sanitary system.

Waldo Adams met us at the Old Colony [The remaining text of December 11 is cut out.]

December 14. Thursday.

Spent the day with Frank Tyler, & Miss Kate told me about her Norway trip.

December 15. Friday.

Lunch at Frank Tyler's, & then we girls, (aunt Patty Gale is as much a girl as any of us), went to Belmont to visit May Goodridge in her new home, on Waverley street. "Will" was away, but May & her mother gave us cordial greeting, & for several hours, we pervaded the house – a jolly party. It is the sunniest little home imaginable, & stands on a hill commanding a beautiful view. May has grown thin, [The remaining text of December 15 is cut out.]

December 17. Sunday.

Went with Emily to Parker Memorial Hall to hear John Weiss. – Dined with Lucy Taylor.

December 20. Wednesday.

Spent the day at the Blind Institution. To my amazement, found Percy in the printing office, feeding the press, & looking as if she had never been away. They are printing Dr. Howe's Memorial. – Nell Peterson came up to spend the day with me, & I made her sit in a sunny window that I might see the golden gleams in her auburn hair. Saw Miss Moulton & Miss Plummer. Came in town with Frank Kilbourne & we went Christmas shopping.

96

December 23. Saturday.

Walked down town just night to see the Christmas holly & evergreen & gay holiday goods. – Emmie and Frank went to the Cape.

December 24. Sunday.

Emily & I went to Kings Chapel & heard Mr Foote. The beautiful old church was green & fragrant as the woods with its Christmas garnishings. We sat with Thackeray's Colonel Newcome. His other name, though, was Sewell Tappan, judging from the lettering of his prayer book. He was a fine looking man, & most courteous to us. – In P.M. I called on Addie Hutchison, Annie Handy's friend.

December 25. Monday.

We went to Mr Hale's church this morning, heard Dr. Bellows, & beautiful Christmas music, & saw Mr Chaney for a few moments. I went to Frank Tyler's & bade them all goodbye. - This is the quietest Christmas I ever spent. We sat alone this evening. Nettie, Emily and myself, the children being at the Cape, & even Joanna was away, the house very still. At first, it seemed lonely, but I went to the window, & there the beauty of the Christmas night made me glad. It was the perfection of a winter night; no wind, the earth packed hard & even with snow, and a flood of moonlight pouring down upon the whiteness. I heard the merry tinkle of sleigh bells, & joyous singing in the distance. A carol party, doubtless. I returned, somewhat cheered, to the quiet room & the enjoyment of Thackeray's "English Humorists."

December 26. Thursday.

Goodbye to Boston. Old Colony Depot at 4 P.M. I bought the latest "Atlantic," took my seat in the train, hedged myself in and people out with a great handful of prickly holly, & gave myself up to the pleasure of reading H.H.'s description of "A Colorado Road." That finished, I turned my attention to the New England landscape. A soft white depth of snow stretched unbroken all the 90 miles from Boston to Brewster. Through this we swept on into twilight & the night, a still, moonless night, lit only by the whiteness of the earth, its hush of snow broken only by the sweet jangling of sleigh bells & pleasant confusion of voices at each station. I leaned my head against the window pane, & enjoyed the succession of snow pictures: the pure levels of field & marsh; the low, softly rounded hills with their guardian pines showing black against their whiteness; the delicate tracery of elms & other deciduous trees against the pale sky; the white mystery of the great snow covered ponds; the cheery glimmer of home lights in the towns & villages through which we passed. We went through Bridgewater in the gathering twilight & the dreamy beauty of its white streets under the graceful elms & the blaze of light from the many windows of Normal Hall were a strong temptation to me to stop, knowing that one of those windows opened into Miss Woodward's room. It was the hour before tea & I could see the girl students resting & chatting merrily in their rooms, & in one corner room that sunshine of smile & glance that I know so well. I sighed to have to leave it behind, but my own home & mother were the stronger magnets. These home comings are so dear, & this was no exception.

Books read in 1876

Gunnar	Boyesen
Memoir of a Brother	Thomas Hughes
Schooldays at Rugby	" "
Tom Brown at Oxford	" "
Antony Brade	Robert Lowell
Heroes & Hero Worship	Carlyle
Life of Prescott	George Ticknor
Marjorie's Quest	Jeannie T. Gould
Sights & Insights	A.D.T. Whitney
Ten Times One is Ten	E.E. Hale
Ups & Down	" " "
Two Years Ago	Charles Kingsley
Silver Pitchers	Louisa Alcott
Three Proverb Stories	" "
For Summer Afternoons	Susan Coolidge
Sintram	Fougue
Queen Mary	Tennyson
Vicar of Wakefield	Goldsmith
Margaret	Sylvester Judd
Memoirs of Celebrated Female Sovereigns	Mrs Jameson
The Bigelow Papers	Lowell
Idylls of the King	Tennyson
English Humorists	Thackeray
The Haunted Man	Dickens
Christmas Carol	"

Volume II

1877

January 9, 1877 through December 31, 1877

January 9. Tuesday.

Theo left us today for his second sea voyage.

January 15. Monday.

Nellie Mullen came to be our "help." – a pretty, sweet-tempered girl.

January 16. Tuesday.

It rained last night & today is cold. At sunset, the under side of every twig and branch & pine needle was hung with transparent ice drops. Through these the sun shone, but there were no prismatic colors, & each drop kept its colorless brilliancy. The distant trees seemed clothed in silver mist, – a lovely effect. I walked to the pines. The grass was thinly plated with ice that crackled delightfully under my feet; even the fence mosses were iced.

January 18. Thursday.

Afternoon with Relief. Little Alice came running to welcome "Miss Caddie," and put up her rosy mouth for a kiss. I am glad she begins to watch for my coming. There are few gifts sweeter than the love of a child freely given. Relief says that whenever a gift or dainty is sent her, Alice thinks it must come from either Santa Claus or Miss Caddie. What an honor – to be ranked with Santa Claus in a child's estimation!

Our Shakspeare Club, reorganized last Thursday, met this eve with Ida Winslow. The reading was miscellaneous, & there were six readers – Alice Crosby, Ida W., Clara Freeman, Mr Dawes, Mr Coffin & myself – and twelve listeners. The officers this year are President – Mr Dawes; Vice Pres. – Mr Snow; Secretary – Mr Coffin; Ass't Secretary – Caro A. Dugan; Prompter – Judy Crosby.

January 19. Friday.

A spring day in the midst of winter. Aunt Olive and I walked to the shore, enjoying the sunshine & mild air. Between the beach & the Great Bar was a field of snow & ice, beyond which was the open sea. Near shore, the close packed ice cakes had broken a little, giving here & there a gleam of blue water. All along the shore the waves had thrown up a solid breast work of snow & ice. – The bayberry bushes were almost bare of fruit. I suppose birds must eat the spicy gray berries. Not a bird was visible today, & no cry of gulls came from back of the Bar.

January 22. Monday.

A quiet snowstorm. Great, moist flakes falling that lay along the tree branches like ermine & spread a thick carpet over the brown earth. I went out just night into the stillness that comes in the wake of such a storm, & it was like walking into a dream. – Mr Coffin came this eve to choose with me a play for the Shakspeare Club.

January 25. Thursday.

Cold & Windy. Shakspeare Club met with Mr Dawes. Read "King John."

January 27. Saturday.

Managers meeting at the Library to plan for an exhibition. Ida came home with me to tea, to talk matters over, we two being committee on dramatic entertainment.

January 28. Sunday.

Aunt Olive & I called at Alice Crosby's this eve. Found Capt. Charles Freeman and wife on our return.

January 31. Wednesday.

Aunt Olive walked with me up Cannon Hill this morning to get the lovely view of town and bay. It was all lovely – the southern reach of brown fields & young pines, the elastic gray mosses of the hillside, the rocks – lichen-colored – that crown the hill, with red stemmed bushes growing out of crack & fissure. Rose bushes these, and the pink wild roses will add another grace to the gray rock next summer.

February 1. Thursday.

The Club met with me. Twenty two present. We read Richard II.

February 3. Saturday.

A light snow fell in the night, and the sun is warm this morning. I coaxed mother up to the house top to see the morning glory. The Bay was heaped with great cakes & ridges of snowy, beautiful ice – no water visible; the pond was thinly spread with ice, looking as if its steel-blue had been dimmed by a breath; here & there amid the silvered brown of the fields, gleamed a rain water pool, bluer than the sky; the pines had shaken off the snow, but along the road the silver abeles flashed with water jewels, and red rose branches were strung thick with the clear drops; Scargo hill was misty & blue in the distance beyond the purple swamps and across the wet roofs of the village drifted the gray mist of smoke born of snow & sunshine. Our great barn roof looked like dark velvet seen through this rolling smoke. It was hard to leave the house top & come down into the busy Saturday morning.

February 5. Monday.

Walked to the cross roads. Found green mosses by the roadside, & gathered a handful of rose haws that burn on in spite of ice & bitter winds & warm the snowy roads.

February 8. Thursday.

Afternoon with Relief. We read Don Quixote. Shakspeare Club in eve at Capt William Freeman's. Twenty eight present. Read the first part of Henry IV. Mr Snow was a capital Falstaff.

February 11. Sunday.

Mild and Sunny. Ida Winslow came home with me from church, & after dinner we drove to Dennis to see Raynor about music for the dance which will close our Library exhibition. Home via West Brewster, stopping to lunch at Mrs Nath'l Winslow's.

Winslow House & Mill Pond

February 25. Sunday.

A driving rain & east wind. Steenie & I walked to the shore just night, in the teeth of the storm. The water was gray & wild, & "the blinding mist came pouring down," hiding the lights of the town & shut [next lines cut from diary.]

March 1. Thursday.

Relief was very quiet today. She is not so well this winter.

March 8. Thursday.

The usual quiet afternoon in Relief's little room. She had a handful of English violets beside her, a gift from Addie Nickerson.

March 13. Tuesday.

Aunt Mame came home. The snow is falling, moist & light enough to make a lovely sight of the tangle of leafless vines & dry flower stalks by the roadside. Like fairy architecture are the delicate snow arches and slender columns that I kneel to examine. [lines cut from the diary.]

today; pinks, orange blossoms, tea roses. Her face is sweet to look upon when enjoying her flowers, & no blossom is fairer than the little hand that touches them so lovingly. – The Shakspear Club met with Dr. Gould this eve, for a miscellaneous reading. Mr Dawes gave two laughable parodies on Longfellow's "Excelsior," & a remarkable discourse on the sin of wearing a periwig, by Parson: Weeks, who lived in Harwich 150 years ago. Aunt Mame read "Skipper Ireson's Ride." And Dr. Gould told us that his father when a little boy was riding out from Salem on that day, and met the procession of Marblehead women, with the cart in their midst, and while he gazed, old Ireson was set free, and in his wretched plight, sped away up the Salem road. The Doctor also told us about a man whose father had been smothered in a funn(?) of lamp black, and who said to him (the doctor) in telling about it, that he "didn't know when any little thing had tickled him so much!"

March 17. Saturday.

The loveliest snow storm of the season. All night the snow fell, & today we look out upon an enchanted white world. The land is filled with great drifts whose free pure curves are beautiful beyond description; the plu-my evergreen branches, over-laden, bend to the earth; a sea of snow has swept in among the young pines, & here and there a white breaker rears its crest above some brave little tree vainly struggling to free itself. The west garden is full of curious shapes; graceful arches, slender wands furred with snow, a many-fingered skeleton hand waving in the wind like the sea polyps that clutched at Andersen's little mermaid, a white ant-eater climbing a rough tree trunk on whose smallest twig rests a snow cushion many times its size, keeping its wonderful balance despite the rocking North Wind, such is the magical lightness of snow.

March 18. Sunday.

The storm continues, wilder & fiercer today. The air is a mad swirl of snow, the wind shakes their white burden from the trees, only the ever greens holding their own, and keeping their spotless beauty. The long storm in its various phases is a veritable "symphony in white."

March 19. Monday.

Now comes sunshine & blue sky. The eye is blinded by the glory of the white earth and seeks relief in the lovely blue of the snow shadows. Saturday was the "Andant Grazioso" of this white symphony; yesterday both "Maestoso" and "Furioso"; and today is certainly "Allegro con brio."

March 24. Saturday.

A sweet spring morning full of fresh odors and bird songs, the sun shining through the thinnest possible veil of mist. Stephen & I walked to the shore, hunting for my little gold cross, lost in yesterday's sunset walk. It was half tide, and the flats were sunny & brown, the ebbing water blue. The seaweed lay in rich, wet masses at our feet, & off back of the Bar, gulls were calling. We went out to the largest of the rocks lying close in shore – a rock fringed heavily with seaweed & crusted with barnacles, and stood watching the little shell fish clinging to the rock or rolling along like wee Jack tars, with their houses on their backs. I called Stephen's attention to one – "Look at that comical little fellow, he walks like a sailor!" "He is a sailor," said Steenie, smiling down at the tiny shellfish, with much interest.

March 26. Monday.

Twenty-four years old today. Gifts from aunt Dede & Frank Tyler, and mother gave me books – "Schooldays at Rugby" and "Poems" by Barry Cornwall. I called on Ida Winslow in P.M. staid to tea, & we played duets. Win came for me.

March 29. Thursday.

Crocuses have come, & stand in groups in the garden; nodding gaily toward the remains of a big snowdrift over the way. I filled mother's pretty flower scales with them, & carried a handful to Relief. I found flower buds under the leaves on Mayflower Bank, this morning. The grass is vivid green in spots, & buds are swelling on lilac & sweet brier bushes. Salt marsh odors greeted me as I neared Relief's today, invigorating as North wind. The Shakspeare Club met here in eve, to read "King Lear." Mr Dawes was a fine Lear.

March 30. Friday.

The boys are busy in the garden, raking together dead leaves and branches & making a big bonfire. Fine spring work!

April 5. Thursday.

This morning at 8.30 Capt. Solomon Freeman died. He has been gradually failing for a year, running down like a faithful watch worn out with years of service. It has been a painless illness and death, just a slow loss of strength, each day finding the strong-willed old man a little weaker, until he became helpless as an infant before he died. He was like Leatherstocking in his healthy attachment to out of door life and his resolute effort to keep up and about to the very last. He was riding out two weeks before his death, and was up & dressed till within a few days of the end. The night before he really took to his bed, he came staggering out to tea table where the family was assembled, forgetting that he had just had his supper, & disregarding the entreaties of Emma. Tall, gaunt, pale & hollow eyed, the old man appeared among them like a ghost, sank into his accustomed seat, incoherently muttered the grace it had always been his custom to pronounce, & tasted a cup of tea, after which, his momentary strength failed him, & he would have fallen but for the support of his friends.

Mr Dawes, our minister, went in to see him Tuesday morning & was probably the last person Capt. Freeman recognized. The old captain held out his hand, and bowed his head when Mr Dawes said, in his simple impressive way, – "The best word I can give you, my friend, is the sailor's watchword 'Look aloft!'" Later, the feeble thoughts seemed to wander, and he asked Mr Dawes if he wanted to go home; but when the minister repeated a verse or two whose burden was "going home," and the familiar "In my Father's house are many mansions," the old sailor's lusterless eyes again brightened. – This morning his long life of seventy seven years was ended, going out with the ebbing tide.

April 7. Saturday.

Funeral of Capt Freeman this afternoon, to which many people came, forty two carriages following the hearse. Truly, comedy & tragedy are curiously interwoven in this world. Mr Keith, son-in-law of the old captain, a vigorous rather good-looking man, but stupid, narrow-minded & bigoted, was mortally offended because Mr Dawes did not mention him in his prayer. Mr Dawes, hearing of this, said drily [sic], "Did he think the Lord wouldn't remember him without particular mention?" his sense of the ludicrous being keen, tho' he was really grieved that he had been in any way remiss. – The indignation of Mr Keith reached its climax on the way to the cemetery. He & Sophia Freeman, (Horace's widow) were in the Freeman chaise, and, as the horse from lack of exercise, was somewhat inclined to be frisky, Mr E.D. Winslow, who has a huge bump of caution, told Mullen to walk on the side walk abreast of the animal, and keep an eye on him in case he should try any tricks. Poor Mullen, in his eager desire to be of use, quite overdid the business, for out he went into the road & walked at the horse's head! Imagine Mr Keith!! – In the evening, he let off his pent up steam on Mr Winslow who was too honest not to confess his share in the matter.

"As if I didn't know enough to drive a horse! – been a farmer half my life time!" It ended with his saying most grudgingly – to Mr Winslow, "Well, I suppose I must try to forgive you."

April 8. Sunday.

A beautiful sermon from Mr Dawes this morning, with tender & appreciative mention of Capt. Freeman.

April 12. Thursday.

Walter came yesterday for a visit. – Shakspeare Club at Mrs Mary C. Crosby's. Read Antony & Cleopatra.

April 13. Friday.

Walter & the boys drove to the creek to refresh themselves with a sight of Win's boat, & I went with them for a visit to Relief. What an atmosphere of purity and peace pervades her little room! She was full of sorrow at the prospect of losing aunt Nettie. – I saw a picture to be remembered, before coming away. Mrs Howard Winslow called, bringing her baby for a first visit to Relief. She laid the little one in Relief's lap, altho' somewhat apprehensive that the unwonted darkness & the strange face might make her cry, for she is afraid of strangers; but baby May looked with large serious eyes into the sweet face above her, & suddenly put up her soft hand and patted Relief's cheek. The little child, only five months old, seemed to read the heavenly meaning of that face, for again & again she repeated the pretty caress, lying quietly, with her dark eyes uplifted. In the dim light, with their white draperies & pure, pale faces, the little May & my sweet Relief seemed near of kin & very near to heaven. Rosy little Alice danced about, full of joy, rapturously admiring the baby and kissing its dimpled hands. I walked home, enjoying the green grass & picking gray pussy willows.

April 14. Saturday.

Mrs Mayo was buried today, the funeral at the church. She was a dear old lady, one of the old-fashioned kind in person, tall, slender, in straight black gown, cap, black lace mitts & spectacles, minus teeth & wearing her own gray hair; and in character she was most gentle, modest, sweet, & lovable, with an intelligent, sympathetic interest in all affairs of the day, & most of all, in her native town. She longed to see Brewster once more, but submitted to the inevitable without a murmur. Her sister, Mrs Nathaniel Winslow, went up to Boston to see her, carrying some Indian meal, because Mrs Mayo fancied that "gruel made from meal that came from Brewster would be so much nicer." Her illness was short & almost painless. Her grand child, twelve year old May, is a great comfort to Augusta.

Little Maggie Murphy sent me a bunch of may flowers, today.

April 19. Thursday.

Raining, & no Shakspeare Club. I went over to see Alice at 5 P.M. & she gave me a nosegay of geranium leaves, & delicate white flowers from her wax plant. It was a joy to be out in the rain, to inhale the fragrance of the wet earth, and see the tender green of the young grass. One grass sod laden with rain drops, I knelt to examine. Many of the green blades seemed crusted with silver, so thick crowded the tiny drops, & on others the little crystal globes were strung at even distances as tho' the grass blade were part of a rosary.

April 20. Friday.

A misty morning, the grass lightly silvered with yesterday's rain. I went to Mayflower bank, where were many buds were & a few pink &

white blossoms, full of dewy fragrance. Also found new shoots of trailing ground pine. The water rippled over the cranberry swamp and occasionally I heard the dip of an oar & saw the shadowy outline of a boat over across the pond, through the thin veil of mist. I came home through the pines. Each pine-needle was tipped with a clear, pear-shaped raindrop, & bright-eyed birds hopped fearlessly about under the protecting branches. I looked over the fence into Capt. Freeman's grove, where the crows were having a lively discussion – town meeting, perhaps. The trunks & lower limbs of his pines were shaggy with moss, which gave a misty, unreal look to the grove. The fence rail on which I leaned, rested in a post that was rich in mosses & lichen. The green mosses were mostly smooth & fine; the crimped edges of the coarser gray lichen were set thick with fine black hairs like the fringe of a baby's eyelid.

The crocuses are giving place to blue myrtle (or periwinkle) blossoms in the garden, and the trumpet daffodil is in its glory. I spent the day with Relief & walked home at sunset. Its light glorified the branches of the willows behind the weather-beaten Paine house, as I passed, making their golden network into a halo above the dark old roof.

April 24. Tuesday.

Alice Crosby walked with me to East Brewster. An errand took us to the black smith's shop which was empty & silent, the floor strewn with rusty flakes of steel, but in a moment, Mr Ben Crocker's gray hair & ruddy face appeared at a side door. We also went to the house of Mr Harden, house painter, & his daughter, pretty Lizzy Harden, came to the door. "Pretty" is hardly the word; she is something more than that. I fancy Titian would have been glad to paint her, so rich is the gleam of her auburn hair, so brilliant the coloring of lips and cheeks, so clear & soft the warm brown of her eyes. Her hair is brushed back from her face in loose shining waves, and falls in soft curls far below her waist. Her name ought to be Garnet, from the glow in her hair & eyes, lips & cheeks. She has been absent from the Shakspeare Club of late, & I miss her, it is such pleasure to look at her. She is quiet modest & gentle-mannered, & her face is sweet & thoughtful enough for a Madonna. – We called on Hitty Crosby, Abby Crosby, & returning, on Hannah Collins, & dear Dr. Gould. It was warm & sunny when we started, but returned wrapped about by one of our sudden Cape fogs.

April 25. Wednesday.

The perfection of an April day! From my open window, and later, in the warm sunshine out-of-doors, I drank in deep draughts of the delicious air. The dear & beautiful world! how can we help but love it? No wonder "God saw that it was good."

April 26. Thursday.

Down to May flower bank this morning. Along the narrow foot path – the pines whispering above me on one side, the water gently plashing on the other, and tossing light flakes of foam at my feet – I walked slowly often pausing to brush away dead leaves & peer into the ground network of evergreen & moss for hidden treasures. Now a white mayflower would look fearlessly up from between my feet, just in time to save its innocent life, and then I would have a glimpse of rosy color in the midst of a tangle of green, and brushing away leaves & fresh ground pine, my fingers would dive into a bed of wet moss and bring up lovely clusters of shy, pink blossoms. "Oh you darlings!" I would cry, & then another flower would peep at me from under the leaves, and so they drew me on, step by step, until my basket was full. – Shakspeare Club at Hitty Crosby's this eve, & readings from Longfellow. A glorious moonlight eve.

April 27. Friday.

"Gay little Dandelion
Lights up the meads,
Swings on her slender foot,
Telleth her beads."

The first one of the season is here nestling in the grass that grows green by the front door. The garden bank is blue with periwinkles, and the purple hyacinth is in bloom. I walked to Relief's & Alice accompanied me. Read "Julius Caesar."

May 5. Saturday.

Walked to the shore with Steenie this morning. He went flat fishing, & I lay down on a sunny rock & watched him make his way over brown flats & blue channels, in his long fisherman's boots, with trident over his shoulder. Two men were already far out on the sands, on the same errand, standing motionless, with watchful eyes bent on the rippling water. I lingered awhile on the beach, then climbed the bank & went

Breakwater Beach

home, gathering on the way, fresh green leaves of the beach pea, the small reddish bayberry buds, as fragrant now as the leaves will be later.

May 8. Tuesday.

Walked to Relief's after dinner, taking the short cut across the dike. A low bank beyond Capt. Freeman's was white with wild strawberry blossoms; dandelions, young clover leaves, & the fresh coral of sorrel brightened the ground; pussy willow waved its gray wands, and near Alice's home, the tansy was green and thick as parsley. On low, wet ground near the dike, ferns were throwing back their warm gray hoods, huckle berry bushes were pink with swelling buds, and delicate fair anemones were trembling on their slender stems. – Later in the afternoon, Nettie came down to give Relief some music, & I drove with Emily meanwhile, through the Dillingham road and round by the Brook.

May 9. Wednesday.

I made dresses for Emmie's paper dolls. The child is as busy & interested as if she were to be here all summer instead of a few days. She has made a small garden for herself, transplanting tulips & myrtle; a stable for her "black horse" Duke, with manger, chain, etc. & three little wagons which she painted red & black. She has been very happy with Duke, feeding, currying & harnessing him every day, & driving him with pink flannel reins over his black back!

May 11. Friday.

Lola and Baby Bangs, Mr & Mrs Collins called. Albert & Grace Taylor came in eve train.

May 12. Saturday.

Albert & Grace returned to Boston in P.M. – Last Shakspear Club of season at Mary C. Crosby's. Read Tennyson and had a pleasant, social time.

May 13. Sunday.

A lovely hazy day. Mr Dawes spoke of Nettie's approaching departure and read a little poem "Goodbye."

This P.M. I went over to the other house and helped pack. Nettie rode down to bid Relief goodbye. Dr. Gould & wife, Mr Dawes, Zoeth Snow & wife, aunt Olive and Mr Winslow all called today. I put little Emmie to bed for the last time.

May 14. Monday.

Emily & Walter went in early train, and Nettie & the child at noon.

May 15. Tuesday.

Flowers! Violets blue & white, peach blossoms flushing the bare brown twigs, cherry blossoms, maple sunshine in the avenue, yellow celandine in crevices of stone walls, & white sprays of shad bush in the swamps. The willow waves golden branches, & the abeles are a soft, silvery gray, while the fresh green of young elm leaves is like a spring carol.

May 16. Wednesday.

Nettie, Emmie & Walter sailed this morning for England, on way to South Africa, in the steamer Utopia.

In P.M. I went through the swamp road with Alice. Found plenty of anemones hid in the briery thickets, one half opened bell wort, pale yellow, hanging its pretty head, young ferns unrolling, the deep rose pink of leaflets on the wild grape vine, abundant white bloom of shad bush, & the shining leaves & long, graceful aments of the white or poplar-leaved birch.

May 17. Thursday.

I drove to the Brook at sunset with Win and Bessie. A lively scene. Men, horses, barrels, baskets, barefoot boys, dogs, dancing water & fluttering, frightened, silvery herring.

May 18. Friday.

I went out back of the orchard this morning, under the fresh green of the Balm of Gilead trees, & into the meadow gay with dandelions, & cinquefoil. Here also were white violets & abundance of strawberry blossoms, to be remembered later. I went to Fern Thicket. On its field border, crowded strawberry blossoms, dandelions like little suns, fine white mouse ear, white violets, & cinque foil, golden & compact. On the water border, the strip of sandy margin was edged with foam & green with moss, & very near the water ventured the violets & ferns as if going hand in hand, for a bath. Far off, above the rote of the sea, I heard the warning fog horn, for the water was shrouded with fog. In the heart of the thicket are ferns – whole families of them! – and today the elder ones were stretching their slender limbs & shaking out their green spring robes, although the very young, the fern babies, were still closely hooded. Here too were groups of anemones, and Solomon's seal in bud.
– In our garden, tulips are opening, yellow jonquils waving, lilies of the valley hiding under broad green leaves, currant bushes hanging out pale green blossoms, & pear blossoms opening red hearts to the sun. First come the rosy peach blossoms, & then in succession the cherry, the pear, & the apple veil themselves in beauty. At the east end of garden stands a balsam fir, now full of little rosy & purplish cones, looking as if it had been dipping its fingers in a strawberry bed.

May 25. Friday.

A dash out in the rain after apple-blossoms, getting my sleeve wet through in the attempt. Found pink flowering almond and green sprays of money-wort. – The beach plum is in flower along the roadsides, its leaves young and scarce unfolded, but the stiff twigs & branches completely hidden in snowy bloom, the flowers being not unlike smaller cherry blossoms. Buttercups, too, are here.

May 28. Monday.

Stephen, aunt Mame & I took an early drive, going through the swamp road that I might gather Solomon's seal, & starry blossoms of chick weed winter green. Later, I went over to the other house, to get fragrant crab apple blossoms, & pretty ground ivy or Gill over the ground, which is abundant under the great horse-chestnut trees, & a branch of maple, for its curious green keys. – At sunset, Stephen & I drove to the Brook, taking Alice Crosby for her first sight of the herring catch. Crazy Nat, a boy of fourteen, was standing barefoot in the water among the slippery herring, & the men on the bank were chaffing & laughing, trying to get him to bite off the head of a live fish, which he is sometimes prevailed upon to do.

May 29. Tuesday.

Mother went to Boston to attend the May meetings. – The horse chestnuts are in magnificent flower.

May 30. Wednesday.

Little May Bangs was here this morning and we went to Fern Thicket together. She is a charming little companion on a walk, so quick is her observation, so ardent her love for flowers. I could hardly win her from the white violets in the meadow by promise of fairer flowers beyond, & she was quite indignant that I should prefer any to her little favorites. – Fern Thicket was full of soft light and shadow. We found there white choke berry blossoms, winter green and Solomon's seal, polygonatum – a graceful spray of leaves with slender green flower bells strung along the under side of the stem, and white bell-shaped flowers of the huckleberry. We also found a natural flower vase formed of nine great branching ferns, which I christened the May vase in honor of its little discoverer, who was herself the prettiest sight, sitting beside it, with waving ferns all about her, and sunshine glinting down through green boughs & bringing out the red and gold gleam of her hair. – This afternoon, Steenie & I carried Relief a May basket. It was made of blue & white tissue paper (Steenie's handiwork) and filled with flowers and gifts. Relief's pleasure was lovely to see, and also Steenie's delight in watching her. He is one of her weekly readers now, a good thing for them both.

The roadside was gay with wild geraniums and I found the star-flowered Solomon's seal with its many leaves & single white cluster of blossoms. The Star of Bethlehem is in bloom at our own door.

112

May 31. Thursday.

Steenie & I went flat fishing this morning far out on the breezy flats. He waded into the deep channel, speared the fish, one by one, strung them on a long line, and trailed them after him through the water. – I found yellow wild oxalis in the fields, and purple beach peas on the beach.

June 1. Friday.

Bessie, Stephen & I drove to Harwich this morning, & B. & S. had their pictures taken. Steenie brought me blue flag & white horse radish & red clover today.

June 3. Sunday.

In P.M. we (Win, Stephen, aunt Mame & I) drove through East Harwich woods. Wild lupine made great patches of brilliant blue in open places.

June 4. Monday.

Mother came home, & aunt Lucy Parks with her.

June 7. Thursday.

Walked to Relief's. Found the first wild strawberry and in the rank grass of the dike, white blossoms of side-flowering sandwort & the small purple march pea.

June 19. Tuesday.

Unitarian Conference here. We had for guests, Lizzie Munroe, Mr Simpkins & a Mr Thatcher.

June 20. Wednesday.

The family are in high glee over Mr Thatcher – his many questions, his marked attention & compliments to mother. He is very unconventional, doubtless owing to his lack of home & near kin, & to a long invalidism – eight years confined to his bed with some spinal trouble. Mother asked him to stay another day, and he accepted with cheerful alacrity. In P.M. we went out on the flats, narrowly escaping a thorough wetting by the returning tide. The beach was bright with yellow flowering poverty grass & we found the beach pea and red laurel. The pale pink arethusa, which Hawthorne calls "one of the delicatest, gracefullest, and in every manner sweetest of the whole race of flowers," is in bloom by the pond, in the wet moss under azalea bushes.

June 21. Thursday.

White deutzia blooming in the garden. Wild roses make beautiful the road to Relief's, & I found there today the delicate flower cups of the Rutland beauty, or wild morning glory. This is a vine which winds in & out of the wayside bushes. A budded spray of it lasts for a week in water, when gathered, each morning a fresh pink blossom opening to live for a day.

June 22. Friday.

Today, went with Thorwald & Charlie to the pond. Gathered arethusa & wild honeysuckle, cranberry blossoms, & the first yellow flowers of St. John's wort with its curious punctured leaves. In the evening we went to the shore to see the unusually high tide which came up under our bath house, rocking it like a boat. It was wild & eerie – the strong wind, and the black rushing waves with their foamy crests & flying spray.

Delicate sweet brier roses are in bloom, and the money wort shows its gold. Black alder hangs out tiny white blossoms, the thistle is clothed royally in purple, the gray field "pussies" (stone clover) are here, & mallows with its store of pretty lavender blossoms & promise of "cheeses."

June 23. Saturday.

A letter from Theo. Emily came tonight.

June 26. Tuesday.

Visited Relief. Yellow loosestrife in flower, yarrow, many of whose white flowers are stained a lovely pink, yellow star grass, butter & eggs, marsh marigold's "barbaric gold," crimson grass pinks, & white elder flowers.

June 27. Wednesday.

Tiger lilies are burning bright under the smoke tree. Charlie & I walked to the pond just night & gathered a handful of arethusa (which I carried to Addie for her sister Mrs Myra Nickerson to paint), & filled a basket with fragrant swamp honeysuckle, now in its glory. – Frank Kilbourne came in evening train.

June 28. Thursday.

Ida Winslow's school picnic today. I went with her according to promise, and Frank Foster & Tully Crosby were active helpers, putting up a swing, making lemonade, &c. We camped in a pine grove on a hill overlooking the east end of Long pond. The children had a good time. They all love Ida, and she has them under perfect control. She had spared no pains to make their holiday pleasant – bringing up ice for lemonade, making two great loaves of frosted cake sprinkled with candy, & a big basketful of sandwiches. She joined in their plays & was merry & interested yet with no loss of dignity. The picnic dinner was a marvel of orderly behaviour – the children seated in a circle around the cloth, every eye fixed on the goodly array of food, but all waiting patiently to be served, & eating quietly like children who had been well trained in table manners. They waited (altho' very hungry, for dinner was rather late), each child holding a mug of lemonade & a cracker, until all were served, the last helping being the signal for a vigorous onslaught. Ida filled a plate with the cream of the goodies for little Maggie Murphy, thinking it "good for the children to remember their sick playmate," & placed it in the centre of the table, asking the children if they would like to send it to Maggie. There was general & hearty assent. – Little Bennie Tubman drank a fabulous number of mugs of lemonade & swallowed a tin whistle on top of that! – It was a pretty picnic & I like Ida all the better for this day with her & her children.

June 29. Friday.

Mother sold the Copeland place to Frank Foster.

July 11. Wednesday.

Harry Murphy drove up the yard this morning, with little Maggie who looked like a spirit, so white & frail. She brought me a nosegay of poppies & geraniums, and I gave her a lapful of waterlilies cool & fresh from the pond, while mother brought out to her some sugar cakes.

July 12. Thursday.

Frank & I took tea at West Brewster. Ida Winslow came down for Frank to tune her piano, & insisted upon my driving back with her also. It is a pleasant old-fashioned homestead, & the people are so cordial & hospitable that I like to go there. Little Aggie Foster did the honors of garden & swing & cow-house, and I took a walk by the ponds with Ida, seeing blue pickerel weed.(Ida called it "punk") growing in the water and a golden glory of loose strife in the rippling water shallows. We came back to Ida's garden, & she gathered for me a nosegay of sweet scented flowers, with abundance of heliotrope.

July 14. Saturday.

Ida went bathing with us. She looked very pretty in her gray flannel dress, with her curls caught back in a Psyche knot, but the shock of the cold waves made her shiver, the swaying tossing motion brought dizziness, & her lips were "a dark navy blue" to quote Emily. She was game however & declares she will try it again. – Wild indigo is in yellow blossom, & I bring its great, spreading bushes home to fill our largest vase. Milkweed shows sunburnt grace by the wayside. Old maids' pinks sweeten the air & their delicate pink is a color not to be despised. Pink plumes of hard hack by the pond, are beginning to show.

July 19. Thursday.

A long afternoon with Relief, for the rain came & kept me there until 8.30 when Thomas brought me home. We had a dear bit of talk in the twilight. I believe we grow nearer & dearer to each other with every meeting.

July 28. Saturday.

An afternoon with Relief. – The button bush is covered with round white blossoms & the tansy gold begins to show. Everlasting is fresh & white, yellow primroses open large & sweet along the roadside, & succory hangs out delicate blue flowers on an unsightly, straggling stalk.

July 31. Tuesday.

I helped the children give impromptu charades & tableaux this eve, much to their delight, as they were wandering about in rather aimless fashion. We had the "Babes in the Wood" with Josie Stallknecht & Herbert Kneeland for babes, lying on a waterproof & several handfuls of grass, while little Charlie was the robin, with scarlet flannel breast & waterproof-cape wings, hopping about & dropping a big grape leaf on

116

each babe. Next the execution of Mary, Queen of Scots. Herbert was Queen Mary in long water proof cloak and paper ruff, with his head on the block (a stool), and a very pretty Queen Mary was he, with his fair face, light hair & small features. Thorwald was the headsman with an ax & a fierce frown, & Josie & I were the weeping maids. We also acted "rhapsody" & "rampage" & "pupil."

August 3. Friday.

Addie Nickerson took me a drive to Cliff pond this P.M. The woods were fresh & green, owing to frequent rains. Slender sprays of golden rod begin to show along the grassy wood roads.

In our cranberry swamp the white Clethra is overpoweringly sweet, the meadow beauty shows its rosy petals & yellow stamens like little tongues of flame, jewel weed hangs flowers of orange gold against dark green leaves, the grass pink still lingers, & we see white spirea faintly tinged with rose.

August 4. Saturday.

Anna found a beautiful flower on the margin of Long pond, – like a small wild rose & of lovely rose color, with a golden star-shaped center edged with purple.(Sabbatia)

August 5. Sunday.

Old captain Warren Lincoln fainted in church.

August 8. Wednesday.

Picnic at Jolly's, – just our own family, aunt Olive, Mr Winslow, Bell Keith and Alice Crosby. Win came home last night from his fishing trip, in time to enjoy the picnic. I found it too intolerably hot to find much pleasure out of doors. Stephen gathered me a pretty bouquet of wild flowers, among them the white bell-like blossom of the checkerberry, & the berries of the Solomon's seal, in clusters of five or six, small, pale red sprinkled with deeper red and very pretty.

August 10. Friday.

Today came Capt. Jonathan Nickerson wife & three daughters – Isabel, Florence and Grace – and R. Carter, a young doctor on the staff of the hospital for the insane.

117

August 11. Saturday.

The Nickersons, Emily & myself went up to Addie Nickerson's this evening, where we met the Sears's & Lola Bangs. Had a jolly time playing pantomime.

August 12. Sunday.

A drive to East Harwich this P.M. with Addie Nickerson & her friend Fanny Crosby. Fanny is such a charming little person, it is a pleasure simply to look at her. She is very like Lotta: in face & form & the careless grace of her movements, – being small & slight, with laughing dark eyes, constantly changing expression, and little head covered with soft brown curls. She is very lovable, & seems made to be petted and shielded. – We discussed "Daniel Deronda" at dinner, Dr. Carter defending & upholding Grandcourt.

August 13. Monday.

Addie & Fanny came down in their boating suits for a row, just before supper, – which they did not get, for it rained suddenly – sheets of water, thunder & lightning followed, & they remained to tea, after which "little Fan" sung "Lord Lovel" and other ballads.

August 14. Tuesday.

I made a flying call on Relief in A.M. while I was driving about doing errands for mother, & carried her a handful of pansies from Martha Huckins's garden.

August 15. Wednesday.

Spent day with Ida Winslow at West Brewster. We had planned a drive in the woods & a ramble round the ponds, but it rained all day & kept us indoors. I enjoyed looking over Ida's curiosities, ransacking the great double attic, playing with baby Emma, & listening to little Aggie's quaint talk. The baby is plump, rosy & fair, with a fine carriage of the head, & reigns a little queen. She is so energetic & determined that she often rules her quiet elder sister, for all the five years between them.

August 16. Thursday.

A row on the pond this morning. The water lilies were all open, white & lovely in the sunlight, & I gathered some for Relief, walking down there this afternoon. White asters & purple thoroughwort by the way. The jewel weed is in its prime, & the reed grass begins to shake out its light plumes.

August 18. Saturday.

A lovely moonlight evening which we spent on the pond – Win, Steenie, Thorwald, Isabel, Grace, Florence, Emily & myself. We rowed vigorously for a time, and then floated, an occasional stroke of the oars keeping us well off the shallows. We sung most of the time, a medley of boat songs, patriotic airs, negro melodies & German love songs, and enjoyed the deep shadows and rippling light on the water, the clear [lines cut from the diary].

[Continuation of a date unknown because of the cut page.]

Emily & I went to Nauset with Addie & Priscie Nickerson & Fred Lambert. We had clear sunshine, & a fresh breeze blowing in our faces all the bright fourteen miles of our drive. We had a charming little dinner in a room of the light keeper's house, whose windows looked out on the blue sea & passing vessels, & later, quiet rest & talk on the white sands near the curving line of the breakers. We drove home through the warm golden haze of a perfect autumn day, facing a wonderful sunset sky, which gave place later to clear starlight. Passed a field of [pages cut from diary].

September 13. Thursday.

Relief's birthday. I drove down with Addie & Priscie to carry her gifts and flowers.

September 20. Thursday.

Walked to Relief's through her bright, flowery lane.

November 15. Thursday.

A lovely sunshiny day. Went to see Relief, calling on the way, at the Old Maids' house to leave blancmange for lame Miss Lucy.

December 24. Monday.

Frank K. is here for the holidays & Stephen came tonight. A Christmas party at the Hall this eve, the decorations of ground pine holly & wild cranberry. The stage was especially pretty, with an arch of cranberry vines at the back, beneath which stood a holly tree whose leaves & bright berries glittered in the reflection of numerous little tapers. In front & overhead was a "Star," & "Merrie Christmas" in green lettering. The children sang carols, in which I had trained them, Emily playing for them, & "The cold wind shakes the branches bare," – "Come ye lofty, come ye lowly," – "Joyfully, joyfully, carol Christmas bells," – "The angels sang in the silent night," – "Hark! a burst of heavenly music," – "God rest ye, merry gentlemen," – and "Hark! the angels singing," rang out heartily. Several children recited verses, Mr Dawes was presented with books, & then we had supper and a dance – an old-fashioned Virginia reel in which old & young joined with much gusto.

December 25. Tuesday.

We had a jolly time over our gifts this morning, which were spread out on the piano, - and a merry Christmas dinner. Just night we drove to Relief's carrying a big budget of gifts. The dimly lighted room, the bright faces of little Emmie & Alice, the table covered with gifts, & Relief's sweet face full of happiness made a happy ending to the day. "Such a happy Christmas!" said Relief, "I don't believe any one in town had so many gifts as I, and I am sure no one has so many beautiful friends."

December 27. Thursday.

The loveliest white frost this morning silvered the ground and made fairyland of the interlacing tree branches. I could hardly take time to finish dressing, because of the beauty out of doors. – The Shakspeare Club here tonight for a Christmas reading. Emily read the description of the Pickwickians Christmas sports on the ice, and I read from the "Carol" about the ghost of Christmas Present & the Cratchits Christmas dinner. Mr Dawes said "Nothing should be read after that. Dickens is the great master of all fiction, & other Christmas writing is but an echo of his inspiring words." We closed with a general sing, Frank playing for us "America," "Auld Lang Syne," and Mrs. Howe's "Battle Hymn."

December 28. Friday.

Another white frost, even more exquisitely beautiful than the last, for the light crystals melted and dripped from the trees, and the morning sunlight striking through them brought out flashing rainbow colors.

Books read in 1877

Memoir of Dr. Howe	Mrs Howe
Mercy Philbrick's Choice	H.H.? [sic]
Bits of Talk	H.H.
Boys of Other Countries	Bayard Taylor
A Painter's Camp	Hamerton
Thomas Wingfold Curate	MacDonald
Two Years Before the Mast	Dana
White as Snow	Edw. Garrett
Winter Sunshine	John Burrough
Recollections of a Literary Life	M.R. Mitford
Rose in Bloom	Louisa Alcott
Water Babies	Chas. Kingsley
American Note Books	Hawthorne
French & Italian Note Books	"
A Double Story	MacDonald
Twice Told Tales (2 vols.)	Hawthorne
That Lass O'Lowrie's	Burnett
Cape Cod	Thoreau
Deirdre	[No author given]
Gen. Butler in New Orleans	Parton
Italy	Sam'l Rogers
My Little Love	Marion Harlan
The Heroes	Chas. Kingsley
A Blot on the Scutcheon	R. Browning
Judas Maccabaeus	Longfellow
Mabel Martin	Whittier
Wych Hazel	Susan Warner
The Gold of Chickaree	" "
Lessons in Proverbs	Richard Trench
Hist. of Civil War (3 vols.)	Draper
Daniel Deronda	George Eliot
Hetty's Strange History	H.H.? [sic]
Kenneth	Yonge

Life & Letters of Macaulay (2 vols.)	Trevelyan
Life of Sydney Smith	Lady Holland
Letters of Sydney Smith	edited by Mrs Austin
Battle of Gettysburg	Sam'l P. Bates
Pictures of Europe	C.A. Bartol
Don Quixote	Cervantes
Dombey and Son	Dickens
John Brent	Theodore Winthrop
Waiting for the Verdict	R.H. Davis
A Princess of Thule	Wm. Black
Twelve Miles from a Lemon	Gail Hamilton
A Shabby Genteel Story	Thackeray
Two Hundred Years Ago	[No author given]
Christmas Carol	Dickens

1878

January 8. Tuesday.

A dramatic entertainment & dance at the Hall, to raise money for the Library. We gave "The Spirit of '76," the actors being Win & Mr Wentworth, Emily, Lola, Ida Winslow & myself. We have had some jolly rehearsals this last week & are almost sorry these are ended. In addition to the drama, Mr Dawes read, & Mr King supplied music. We barely escaped a panic as the footlights set fire to the curtain, making a lively blaze, but prompt action extinguished it in a few moments. Lola looked very pretty as "Victorine," the scarlet of her hunting suit being most becoming. Mr Wentworth donned a moustache for the occasion, which made him "a raving, tearing beauty" according to Lola. Unfortunately, it dropped off during the second act, much to the amusement of the audience. Emily was capital as Griffin, & Win as Wigfall, tending the baby, while Ida was quite impressive as the Judge, in powdered wig and ermine bordered robe.

January 15. Tuesday.

Afternoon with Relief. Shakspeare Club met with Lola Bangs to read "Taming of the Shrew."

January 17. Thursday.

Another afternoon with Relief, for Sene is away & she is lonely. Universalist entertainment at the Hall in eve, which Emily, Win & I attended.

January 19. Saturday.

Mother went to Boston. Reading at Hall tonight by Prof. Eastty, an English man. We enjoyed especially "The Raven" and "Breaking-up of Dotheboys Hall."

January 22. Tuesday.

Emily & I walked to the shore & home through the pines. The sea was blue & quiet, & the pines quite weird after the rain, their trunks wet & black, & the pale green moss on the dark branches having a mist like effect.

January 24. Thursday.

Pleasant Club meeting at Dr. Gould's. A Longfellow reading, & a social talk afterward.

January 25. Friday.

Went to Relief's. We are reading John Weiss's "Wit, Humor & Shakspeare" with much enjoyment. The clown in "Twelfth Night" says – "The tailor make thy cloak of changeable taffeta, for thy mind is a very opal." It reminded me of Emily.

February 7. Thursday.

The Shakspeare Club met with me, and we read Longfellow's "Golden Legend." Twenty present. The parts were admirably suited to the readers & all did well.

March 5. Tuesday.

A Mother Goose entertainment at Knowles Hall to help pay for the new piano for the Sunday School. It was hard work the getting it up, but most interesting the children were so bright & enthusiastic. Joey Lincoln, May Bangs, Freemie Crosby, Lily Clark & little Aggie Foster were the star performers. Joey was the funniest little "bachelor" imaginable, and May as his wife, was quaint & lovely in white satin & bridal veil. May was also the queen in "Sing a Son of Sixpence," and was fairly brilliant in green silk with a crown on her red gold hair, her black eyes bright with excitement. Freemie was "Simple Simon," playing the fool so naturally that his mother declared she was positively frightened. Lily was a charming BoPeep, in a pretty costume of scarlet & white, with a crook, and wide-brimmed straw hat caught up with bright flowers. Her every motion was full of grace, whether she skipped lightly about, or threw herself down on a heap of ground pine, to fall fast asleep. "Little Miss Muffet" was dazzling. Seated on her "tuffet," dressed in white with scarlet stockings, & a blue & white handkerchief arranged like a pointed cap on her head, with her cloud of golden hair, the deep blue of her starry eyes and rich color in lips and cheeks, little Aggie had never looked more beautiful in her life. The picture was made effective by her unconsciousness & childish abandon, her evident enjoyment of the crumbled bread that served for "curds & whey," also by the contrast this lovely little vision presented to the immense black spider that came dropping down beside her. She was greeted with a storm of applause, which continued till the little scene was twice repeated. The acting was all in pantomime, each verse being represented on the stage as the children or myself sung the words.

March 13. Wednesday.

Mother Goose again, because of the universal desire for its repetition. The programme was changed a little, some things being left out, & new ones taking their place. "Cinderella [sic no closing "] was the most charming addition. I wrote some verses telling the story, & sung them to one of the Mother Goose melodies. Hannah Knowles & Florence Hopkins were the proud sisters, looking very pretty in pink silk & tarlatan. Joey Lincoln was the prince, in black velvet & jeweled orders; Harry Crosby, a grave little herald; Rena Snow, the fairy godmother in scarlet dress, cloak & pointed cap; and Aggie was a dear little Cinderella in brown calico, with a kerchief tied over her golden hair, and later resplendent in white tarlatan, pale blue ribbons, spangled slippers & pearl ornaments. Miss Muffett was of course repeated, & again the little child-star was called out three times, and after Cinderella, she & the little prince came out together and bowed to the audience. It was good to see the interest that all the children took in Aggie – how heartily they joined in the general applause, with what admiring eyes they gazed upon her, & how proud they were of her success. There was no alloy of jealousy in the children's homage, whatever may have been the case with some of the mothers.

March 14. Thursday.

I carried the first crocus to Ida this morning. I go in to see her nearly every day, sometimes finding her quite bright & like her old self; again with the fluttering breath & gray pallor so sad to see. She has grown rapidly worse during her visit to Boston. She is so brave about bearing pain, so resolved to be bright & cheerful, that even now, people hardly realize the extent of her danger. Her disease is the kind of heart trouble accompanied by much suffering, and one does not dread it for her any the less, because she will bear it so heroically.

March 15. Friday.

I carried may flowers to Relief.

May 10. Friday.

A deep water weir has been made for this summer, off by Relief Paine's, and a large ice house & fish house built on the shore by the creek. At high tide, great seine boats go off to the weir, & return laden with fish. Mother & I watched them tonight, when she drove down to the Paines to take me home. The boats came in swiftly, their sails gleaming rosy in the sunset light. The sails were furled as the boats glided into the golden water of the creek, rounded a point of land, and drew up at the little wharf. We could see the fish, the men standing knee deep in the shining, fluttering mass. There were cod, tautog, porgies, and mackerel which the sailors call "the prettiest fish that swim." All (save the porgies which are used for bait only) are packed in ice and sent away in quantities to city markets.

May 27. Monday.

We drove to the Brook at sunset but were too late to see the herring caught so we went down to the creek, reaching it just in time to see the boats come in, gleaming ghostly white in the twilight. There was a big haul of fish and among them a great sturgeon –

_____" the sturgeon Nahma,

Mishe Nahma, King of Fishes."

Some of the men held lanterns while the rest unloaded, and the red lights flashed on the dark wharf & shining fish & rough garb of the fishermen. Old Mr Augustus Paine said such a sight always made him think of the Sea of Galilee and Simon Peter's words "Master we have toiled all the night, and have taken nothing; nevertheless, at thy word I will let down the net." – I made a flying call on Relief, who looked like a white lily in the subdued lamplight.

Herring Brook looking west

127

June 6. Thursday.

Emily & I drove to Orleans, calling on the Seaburys & Doanes. The Doane mansion is a big, old-fashioned house where comfort & hospitality prevail. I was quite charmed with Mary Doane, whose husband Capt. Seth Doane died last year while away from her, traveling South for his health. Her sweet, sad face and the way in which she spoke of her husband, reminded me of Draxy Miller. They made us stay to supper. "It may be a feast or it may be a famine. We vary." said John Doane, "but in any case, you are sure of Martha's coffee." And most delicious was the coffee, with thin slices of bread & butter, and strawberries. Only one box of berries, the first of the season, brought home for a treat, so sharing it with two guests was true hospitality. We drove home by the light of a young moon.

June 20. Thursday.

Ida has been in Boston the last six weeks, to be under the immediate supervision of her physician. She has been worse of late, and today a telegram summoned her sister Mary.

June 21. Friday

Ida's mother sent for. – A letter from South Africa today brought news that uncle Free was very ill, his recovery impossible.

June 22. Saturday.

A letter came from Mrs Knowles, telling me of Ida's great suffering and greater patience.

June 23. Sunday.

I drove to West Brewster to see Emma, who has taken her children up there to keep her father company. The old man sat in the open doorway, seeking consolation in the pages of his Bible. Emma gave me her letters to read, & said that Ida was her brave self, uncomplaining & cheerful. "You are having a hard time," said her doctor sympathizingly, coming in during one of her attacks of coughing & distress for breath. "Oh, it might be a great deal harder," she answered, bravely. Ida tried to reconcile her mother to the approaching separation, saying it was better for her to go now if she could only live to suffer, altho' she was willing to live or die, as the Lord thought best. They must not grieve because she did not give up her school sooner; she loved the work and so kept at it until the last moment, but it could have made no difference.

June 26. Wednesday.

Another letter from Nettie. Uncle Free still living & suffering greatly. She had hardly left his side for twelve days and nights.

July 1. Monday.

I went to Bridgewater this noon. I had little heart for the Biennial, but I had promised Annie Handy I would go. She is ill & going to N.H. for the vacation. Elsie Kelley joined me at So. Dennis & Annie & Ella Handy at Middleboro. I walked up to Mrs Brigg's's pretty new home, with the magnificent Norway spruce before it. Spent evening with Annie.

July 2. Tuesday.

Very hot. Went to see Miss Woodward early, then to Mrs Crocker's for the rest of the morning with Annie. In eve, over to school house.

July 3. Wednesday.

Early call on Miss Woodward. Business meeting at Schoolhouse at 10 A.M. Of the 73rd class, only Mr Boylston, Mr Leonard, Annie, Sadie & I were present. I was with Annie in afternoon, & so lost Miss Woodward's little speech at the collation & the hearty cheering with which it was received. Reunion in eve.

July 4. Thursday.

A last visit to Miss Woodward. Goodbye to the girls at station. Mr King met me at Brewster station and brought news of uncle Free's death. He died very suddenly in Walter's arms at 8 P.M. Friday, the 24th of May. – Today, tho' the Fourth has seemed like Sunday. We walked to the shore at sunset, Hattie B. Mr King, Frank, Emily, aunt Mame and I, and sat on the rocks to watch the lovely changes in sky and water.

July 7. Sunday.

Poor Josiah Winslow was at church. He walked beside me on the way home, & asked about uncle Free. "I thought a great deal of Freeman Cobb," said he. He had a long talk with Steenie, big tears rolling down his cheeks the while. He said people ought to know enough to put their flags at half mast. He had done so.

July 11. Thursday.

A note from Mrs Knowles to say that Ida would like to hear from me, so I sent her a letter tonight. It was a hard thing to do; yet I was glad of the chance of doing anything for her.

July 14. Sunday.

Drove to West Brewster, & carried Aggie some ice cream. Mrs. Knowles went to Boston yesterday, returning in eve. She said that Ida was pleased with my letter and wanted it read again yesterday. They did not believe she could live through the night.

July 18. Thursday.

Ida died tonight.

July 20. Saturday.

The Library was closed today, out of respect for its late Secretary. Emma and her mother, Josephine & George Nickerson, with their sad charge, came at noon, & the funeral was at 3.30 in the West Brewster home. Mr Dawes officiated, & Occa & Angie Crosby, Frank Kilbourne & Mr King sung "Come unto me and I will give you rest," and "One sweetly solemn thought." This last Ida asked May Bangs to sing to her a few days since, & told her mother that she had played it whenever she sat down to the piano last winter, & that she loved the words.

July 23. Tuesday.

Walked to Relief's this afternoon. Asenath gave me a lovely nosegay of heliotrope, & I went in to leave some on Ida's grave when walking home.

July 24. Wednesday.

I drove to West Brewster this evening. They were all sitting in the twilight with open doors – the father & mother Emma & Mary – and very quiet. It was sad, and yet good to be there.

July 27. Saturday.

Library meeting. Resolutions passed on Ida's death. I went to West Brewster in eve to carry the "Resolutions," and the Yarmouth Register of today containing an obituary I had written. Made a flying call as Stephen was waiting for me.

130

July 31. Wednesday.

Priscie Nickerson gave a lawn party this P.M. which turned into a house party, as the weather was bad. There were Orleans people, the Bang's, Sears's, & our folks. We had bowling & billiards, and after supper, games & cards. Supper was served in the parlor at little tables, each seating three or four. A great bowl full of fragrant pink sabbatia stood on the piano, & a dainty nosegay was laid beside each plate. We were served with delicious little biscuit, tongue, salad, olives, coffee, frozen pudding with wine jelly & several kinds of cake. Milly Sears & Cora Nickerson were flying about as waiters, assisted by little "Bobby" Nickerson. They seemed to think it great fun.

August 1. Thursday.

Drove to West Brewster this morning to see Emma and the children.

August 2. Friday.

Picnic at Chatham Lights. The Nickersons & Sears's, Mr E.D. Winslow & Alice Crosby went with us. Hattie Freeman came tonight.

August 3. Saturday.

A morning row on the pond, – Emily, Florence Nickerson, Hattie Freeman & myself. Saw the exquisite little sun-dew in the swamp. Gathered water lilies, pink hardhack, clethra, spirea and bright meadow beauty.

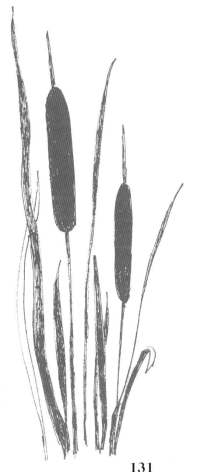

August 4. Sunday.

Little Aggie Foster came from Sunday School with me to dinner. She amused us much by her quaint frankness of talk. Emma came after her just night.

August 5. Monday.

Drove to Cliff Pond with Hattie Freeman & aunt Mary. We found quantities of sabbatia, & also the rose coreopsis.

August 6. Tuesday.

Drove to West Brewster with Hattie and aunt Mame. They went on into the woods, while I stopped for a quiet talk with Ida's mother. Emma & the children left for St. John's this morning to join Frank. Later, we called on Relief.

August 7. Wednesday.

Drove to the woods with Florence this morning. We ate huckle berries and discussed love affairs.

August 8. Thursday.

Went to Relief's where I staid to dinner. In PM. drove to Scargo with mother, Emily, Florence & Hattie Freeman.

August 9. Friday.

At 8 A.M. started for Yarmouth with Mrs Knowles behind Ida's little horse Fanny. We did our several errands, dined at Sears's hotel, & reached West Brewster at 3 P.M. I visited Ida's garden, saw the pansies she planted just before leaving home, & heard more about her last words & farewell gifts. She wanted her glove box given to me, & Mrs Knowles brought it to me today, lying in it some of Ida's gloves & a blue ribbon & lace scarf I had seen her wear recently. Ida showed me this glove box on that rainy August day I spent with her last year, & told me how much she thought of it. – After supper, Mrs Knowles brought me home.

August 12. Monday.

Yellow gerardia & brilliant Turk's cap lilies in the woods. White Lobelia, slender stemmed in the pond. Grace & Isabel Nickerson came. Miss Carrie D. Fuller gave a reading at the Hall tonight, assisted by Miss Clara Seabury. I especially enjoyed her rendering from "Henry V" of the love scene between Henry & Katharine of France. Miss Fuller is an old time teacher of mine, so I had a bit of talk with her after the reading.

August 13. Tuesday.

Mrs Knowles and Addie Baker called. In eve, we were out in the Undine – Grace, Isabel, Winslow, Frank, Nellie, Minot, Emily & myself – singing and floating in the moonlight.

132

August 14. Wednesday.

Hattie Burrill & I went out after lilies this morning, taking Maud, Ally and Bobby Nickerson with us. I went to tea at West Brewster. A lovely sunset of rose & gold. I led Fanny, the little horse, about the yard to eat grass, & coming in played a little on Ida's piano in the twilight, and sung "I am waiting by the river" to Mrs Winslow. Emily came for me, with Grace and Isabel, & we went for a moonlight drive.

August 17. Saturday.

A terrific thunderstorm lasting all night.

August 18. Sunday.

A lovely sunset, with cool sweet air, after the storm. We went for a drive – Frank, Emily, Grace & I, calling at West Brewster to bid Addie Baker goodbye.

August 22. Thursday.

Miss Woodward & her little niece Jeanie Pratt came this noon to visit me. Emily Sears & Alice were here for the day, & in eve we had singing, dancing, conundrums, &c.

August 23. Friday.

Out in the "Undine" this morning – Grace, Jeanie, Miss Woodward & myself. Miss W. tried rowing for the first time with much enjoyment. We found a few late water lilies. We went for a drive this afternoon – Miss Woodward Jeanie & I – leaving Emily at Relief's. We drove to East Dennis & back through the West Brewster hills, to call for Emily. Miss Woodward went in to see Relief a moment, saying a few words to her in a simple heart warm way. She is so like Mrs Whitney's Miss Euphrasia Kirkbright – the same gracious ways of speech, the same heavenly comfort – "going to everything for it, and to everybody with it," the same sweet humility and wide charity. Coming out from Relief's room, we met Elsie Kelley & her sisters at the door. A happy surprise for Elsie to see Miss Woodward. This eve we played the History game. Miss Woodward joins in every game is always ready & interested in trying a new thing.

Beach bathers

August 24. Saturday.

Bathing in A.M. Library in P.M. I roasted corn for the company in evening.

August 25. Sunday.

Rain. Miss Woodward went to church & sat with me in the gallery. Very few present but I enjoyed the service with my friend beside me. We spoke with Mr Dawes, & I could see he was greatly pleased with Miss Woodward. Stephen walked over from Yarmouth this morning, losing his way traveling about nineteen miles. Clear golden sunset that we watched from the housetop. General sing in eve.

August 26. Monday.

Miss Woodward & I took an early drive, going at 5 A.M. to carry Stephen part way to Yarmouth. Miss W. & Jeanie went bathing at 10 A.M. Priscie was here to tea & we tried Clumps and Magnetism & aunt Mame's game. Alice Crosby came to bid me goodbye. She goes with aunt Olive and Belle to Haverhill, N.H.

August 27. Tuesday.

Bathing in A.M. This afternoon, Emily took us (Miss W. Jeanie & me) a lovely drive & new to me. Rather a rough road, up hill and down, but through fragrant oaks and pines, coming out on a fine view of Long Pond & Greenland, where the woods crowded close to the water, & there was a beech grove on a green peninsula, & a windmill on an out-lying hill. Miss Woodward & I were left at the parsonage on our return, where we took tea, in company with Mrs Minot, aunt Mame & Octavia Crosby. Mr Dawes read to us in the evening, some humorous bits. We walked home, star gazing, and found the family guessing "Words."

August 28. Wednesday.

Out in the "Undine" this afternoon – Emily, Grace, Mr King, Jeanie & I – while Miss Woodward went to drive with mother. Jeanie will make a capital little oars woman, she takes to it so readily. Elsie Kelley came to tea. She & Miss Woodward met us as we returned from the boat. This evening we played "Crambo" and "Criticism," Jeanie making some bright hits in the latter game. She is almost painfully shy, (a lameness of seven years obliging her to use crutches, has helped to make her so) and like the evening primrose, slow to open, but when open, so sweet, you wish the flower would never close. She has a real musical gift, playing from memory compositions by Mendelssohn, Gottschalk, &c. with grace and tenderness of expression, and she quite forgets her shyness while at the piano. We could not persuade Mrs Minot to join in our games, but Miss Woodward readily agreed, saying that she believed in entering into everything whether she expected to like it or not, & in that way one could hardly fail to have a "good time" out of it. All times are good to this sweet-souled Elizabeth! Winslow & I walked home with Elsie later.

August 29. Thursday.

Miss Woodward & I spent two hours with Relief this afternoon. Miss W. read a number of John Chadwick's poems & told Relief much about the poet whom she knows well, for he was in the class that entered the first term she taught in Bridgewater Normal School. Relief greatly enjoyed the reading & thought Miss Woodward "beautiful," – said she did not seem like a stranger, but as if she had always known her.

August 30. Friday.

We went to Chatham today, Emily & Grace together, – Isabel & Mr King, Priscie & Mr Thayer, – Miss Woodward, Jeanie & myself. A long warm drive over, dinner on the breezy cliff, - the wide ocean view, deep blue water & gleaming sand bars, a fleet of small vessels tossing at anchor, distant sails & steamers,– a stroll on the wet beach under the clay cliffs and then the drive home. The coast is much changed since last summer; 40 feet of cliff has washed away, & there remains but 28 feet to the old light houses. A long sand bar is making on the right, which it is hoped may serve as a natural barrier; this is formed by the washing away of the coast. An old man whose house, next the light houses on waterside, must be moved this winter, unless the new sand bar proves sufficient safeguard, says he can hardly bear the constant sound of the sea, – it wearies him.

I had a delightful drive home alone with Miss Woodward, for Mr King & I changed carriages, to make it easier for Jane. – Supper tasted good after the long drive. Found that mother had a sharp attack of rheumatism.

August 31. Saturday.

Miss Woodward's last bathing expedition this morning. She went to the Library with me in P.M. & Priscie called there & invited her to drive, then took her into her garden & gathered a bouquet for her.

I had a note from Mrs Knowles saying that she had a quantity of flowers to take to the cemetery, but was unable to go; – would I take them? So I drove to the cemetery after tea, Jeanie & Miss Woodward with me. It was almost too dark to see to arrange the flowers, but we did it after a fashion. Miss Woodward repeated Whittier's lines, as we turned away from Ida's grave.

> "Alas for him who never sees
> The stars shine through his cypress trees!
> Who, hopeless, lays his dead away,
> Nor looks to see the breaking day
> Across the mournful marbles play.
> Who hath not learned in hours of faith
> The truth to flesh and sense unknown
> That Life is ever lord of Death
> And Love can never lose its own!"

September 1. Sunday.

A quiet day, gray & rainy. Isabel went to church with me & helped sing. Mr Thayer preached. – I had a talk with Miss Woodward in her room this afternoon. Mr Dawes called this evening.

September 2. Monday.

Finished marsh rosemary wreaths for Miss Woodward. She planted some butternuts in our west field and gave me some pressed hare-bells, fern & pink daisies, gathered on her mountain trip. I carried her to the station at noon, & bade her & Jeanie goodbye.

Mr King & I went for a row just before tea. Grace & Emily joined us, returning from bathing. Duke plunged in, & seemed to enjoy racing with us. – Isabel and I took a moonlight walk, & called on Elsie Kelley.

September 5. Thursday.

We went up to Priscie's this morning & heard Fan Crosby sing. One sad little song haunts me. It is called "Some Day." – I walked to Relief's in afternoon & had a happy talk with her. Was caught in a thunder shower coming home & thoroughly drenched.

September 6. Friday.

A party at Priscie's this evening. Singing, dancing, games & refreshments.

September 13. Friday.

Relief's thirty-second birthday. I spent the day with her. In the afternoon Amelia Winslow & Betsy Paine came with gifts, – also Addie Nickerson & Fan Crosby, Minnie & Robbie Boyd, Priscie, Lola Bangs & Fred Williams. Mr Williams sung a solo, & a duet with Fannie, "When I know that thou art near me"; Minnie sang some German songs, & Fan sang "Some Day." After these visitors had gone, came aunt Mame & Frank to show Relief the telephone.

September 17. Tuesday.

Sociable at the Library in eve. Frank exhibited his telephone.

September 18. Wednesday.

Frank tuned Ida's piano, & I went with him, at Mrs Knowles's request. She had to go to Boston today. We staid to tea, & Frank played a little to Mrs Winslow. Then we went to Amelia's to tune her piano. Howard brought us home at 9 P.M.

September 19. Thursday.

An afternoon with Relief. This evening Win, Hattie & I spent with Abbie Bangs & Elsie Kelley. Mr Ryder was there & escorted me home.

Sept. 22. Sunday.

No service today. In P.M. Emily & I with Nickersons, took the same lovely wood drive we showed Miss Woodward on Aug. 27. We walked down the hill & into the beech grove where tall, white stemmed trees, thickly interlaced, made a sort of cool green twilight below. – Spent the evening with the Nickerson's & we all – Priscie, Addie, Joe Russell, Addie Lambert, Gus, Emily & I – had a lively discussion on conscience, jealousy, friendship & the temperance questions.

September 23. Monday.

Went to Relief's. We finished "Among My Books." Played crambo at the Nickersons in the evening.

September 26. Thursday.

Began "Paradise Lost" with Relief today. Win came for me & we half filled the carriage with some lovely vines that festooned the roadside bushes with graceful leaves & drooping clusters of pale green seed vessels.

October 1. Tuesday.

Lovely weather. Addie & Priscie N, Emily & I took tea with Lola.

October 3. Thursday.

To Relief in afternoon. First Library sociable in eve. Hard work for us, but quite a success. Singing, logomachy, words, &c.

October 4. Friday.

First rehearsal for Jarley's wax works.

October 6. Sunday.

Emma Foster came home yesterday & I went to see her this eve. She was alone with the children who were most sweet & winning.

October 7. Monday.

Spent the day at Greenland pond – Priscie, Addie, Henry Russell, Win, Emily & I. Carried our boat along & went rowing & fishing.

October 8. Tuesday.

Hattie, Win, Emily & I went to tea with Addie & Priscie. Bowled in afternoon and played art criticism in eve.

October 9. Wednesday.

Called on Emma. The Nickersons here to tea.

October 10. Thursday.

Went to Relief's. Found her father quite seriously hurt. – Second Jarley rehearsal.

October 12. Saturday.

Went up to Emma's in evening, & returning found uncle Alfred here.

October 13. Sunday.

A rain storm yesterday, which increased until at night the wind & rain were terrific. Fences, trees & chimneys blew down, windows & doors were blown in, our Unitarian church steeple was torn off and dropped on the church green, & four vessels came ashore beyond Clark's Point. No lives lost, tho' one man spent the night in the rigging. The north easter continued with almost unabated violence, until ten o'clock this morning. Quantities of lumber came ashore, and the beach was lined with men & teams. Win & uncle Alf got several loads & we (Hattie, Emily, mother & I) went down to see the fun. Priscie & Addie came after. The breakers were fine – a circular sweep of white crests, & single great racing waves that broke on the rocks in showers of snowy spray.

October 14. Monday.

This eve, Emily, uncle Alfred & I went up to the Nickersons & played crambo.

October 16. Wednesday.

Addie & Priscie came this eve to say goodbye. They leave tomorrow.

October 17. Thursday.

Relief & "Paradise Lost." Second Library sociable this eve. Sixty present.

October 18. Friday.

I drove with Mrs Knowles to East Brewster after dinner, leaving her there & bringing back the horse to Emma's. It came on to rain heavily & I spent the afternoon with Emma & the children.

October 21. Monday.

I began with my little scholar, Aggie, teaching her two hours each morning.

October 25. Friday.

Jarley rehearsal this eve at the Hall. Uncle Alfred went over with us, & was much amused.

October 29. Tuesday.

Annie Handy's twenty seventh birthday. I spent the eve with Emma. Made my Indian leggings for Jarley.

October 31. Thursday.

Rainy all day, but cleared at night. Mrs Jarley's Waxworks. We made $23, but would have done better, had weather been more favorable. We have been in a flurry today, hunting up & training another "John," as at the last moment Tully backed out on plea of a cold. Little Aggie went with mother, & greatly enjoyed the performance, especially Von Hillern's walking. Nelly Baker was a lovely "Ophelia," in white, with flowers in her brown hair, and was also very effective as "Niobe," in black with star spangled veil. Frank Snow made a most impressive "Time."

November 1. Friday.

All Saints day. I went up to Emma's in P.M. & took baby out for a walk. – Jarley was repeated this eve to an audience of only twenty one people. $4.20. Bell Atherton came down with uncle Alfred, Thursday eve.

November 5. Tuesday.

Went to see Susie Howard's baby. Found little Aggie there, holding it with great care & satisfaction. Aggie, waking the other morning, saw her mother standing by the crib, with baby's arms clasped round her neck. Aggie gazed a moment, drew a long breath, & said "I do think it would be lovely to be a mother." "Why?" asked Emma. "Oh, to have little children to love you," said the child.

November 6. Wednesday.

The first snow.

November 7. Thursday.

Afternoon with Relief. Evening with Emma.

November 8. Friday.

Alice & Mr E.D. Winslow here to tea.

November 10. Sunday.

Aggie dined with us, & walked with me to the pond & through the pines.

November 11. Monday.

Mother's forty ninth birthday. We all went to drive in P.M. – I took tea with Emma. The children were lovely in their scarlet flannel night dresses & scampered about in high glee. Little Aggie said to me this morning, "I do wish aunt Ida could hear me spell so well."

November 17. Sunday.

Went to church in the rain. Just night carried Bessie Murphy home. She leaves us today and we must be our own Bridgets.

November 19. Tuesday.

Still raining. Went up to Emmas in eve. The children were in bed, but heard my voice, so I had to go up & say goodnight. Baby was especially lovely, lying in her crib, her blue eyes so dark & bright, her cheeks so richly colored, her tiny teeth showing in a mischievous smile.

November 23. Saturday.

Called at Emma's after Library hours, & she kept me to tea, much to the children's delight. They are bewitching in the play hour between supper and bed, playing with blocks, looking at pictures & listening to stories, with eyes, cheeks & hair so bright in the lamplight. – Stephen surprised me by coming to escort me home at mail time.

November 24. Sunday.

Drove with Emma to West Brewster before church. A cool, bright morning after a long week of storm. – Mr Dawes preached Thanksgiving sermon on the text "Are the consolations of God small to you?"

November 28. Thursday.

Thanksgiving day, a gray misty day, clearing at sunset. It was like Sunday, we were so few & so quiet, only Emily, Win, mother & myself. In P.M. Emily & I drove to Relief's to carry a parcel from Addie Nickerson. Relief was also having a quiet Thanksgiving with Thomas, Sene and baby Alice. The gulls were flying in great numbers over the water, uttering wild plaintive cries, & there was a dazzling rift of gold in the cloudy west.

Clouds Over Herring Brook

November 29. Friday.

Went to Emma's to take Baby out for a walk. Brought her home with me where she was highly entertained by the kitten, the birds, and the open fire. Abby & May Bangs spent the afternoon with us.

December 1. Sunday.

Mr Collins preached, & we had an interesting discussion in Bible class on "In whatsoever place, therewith to be content." Mother & I went to drive in afternoon.

December 5. Thursday.

Alice & I went to Relief's.

December 6. Friday.

Sarah Tubman, so young & pretty & useful in her home, died of diphtheria last night, after an illness of three days & was buried today.

December 10. Tuesday.

Emma, Aggie & Mrs Knowles called today, driving up in a pouring rain.

December 18. Wednesday.

Emily & I met Mrs Knowles at Emma's this eve, to catalogue & label the new Library books.

December 19. Thursday.

First meeting of the Shakespeare Club this eve with Mary C. Crosby. Only Mr Dawes, Mr Ryder, Elsie Kelly & myself present. Mr Dawes spoke of Ida, of her faithful attendance & interest in the Club.

December 20. Friday.

I spent the day with Relief.

December 21. Saturday.

Steenie came home for Sunday.

December 23. Monday

Went to the Christmas sale in the Town house this eve.

December 25. Wednesday.

Stinging cold – real Christmas weather. I made an early call at Emma's. In P.M. drove to Relief's with Christmas gifts. On my return, went in to add my bit of green to the Christmas holly, ground pine & rosemary on Ida's grave.

December 26. Thursday.

The Shakspeare Club met with me tonight for a Christmas reading. Alice Crosby came to tea.

Georgie Monroe was buried today.

December 31. Tuesday.

Snow yesterday, but today lovely, sunny weather for this last day of the year.

Books read in 1878

Adventures of Philip	Thackeray
Sights and Insights	A.D.T. Whitney
The Story of Avis	E.S. Phelps
One Year Abroad	Blanche Howard
Faith and Patience	Sophy Winthrop
Autobiography & Letters	Barry Cornwall
Under brush	J.T. Fields
G.T.T.	E.E. Hale
Deephaven	Sarah Orne Jewett
What Career?	E.E. Hale
The Excursion	Wordsworth
Poems. Vols: I, II, III, IV, V	"
Autobiography. 2 vols.	Harriet Martineau
The Turks in Europe	Edward A. Freeman
Brace bridge Hall	Washington Irving
Life of Maximilian I	Frederic Hall
Wit, Humor and Shakespeare	John Weiss
Womankind	Yonge
Tales and Sketches	Hugh Miller
Adela Cathcart	George MacDonald
Songs of Three Centuries	[No author given]
Martin Chuzzlewit	Dickens
Theo	F.H. Burnett
Letter of Charles Lamb (2 vols.)	Sir T.N. Talfourd
Charles Auchester	[No author given]
Life of Mendelssohn	Lampadius
Letters from Italy and Switzerland	Mendelssohn
Charles Kingsley – Life and Letters	[No author given]
Glaucus	Charles Kingsley
Yeast	" "
At Last	" "
Bourbon Lilies	Lizzie Champney
Madcap Violet	William Black
Among My Books – Second Series	Lowell
English & Scottish Ballads – Vols. I, II, III.	[No author given]
Nelly's Silver Mine	H.H.
American Girl Abroad	A. Trafton
MacLeod of Dare	William Black
Peter and Polly	Marian Douglas
Septimius Felton	Hawthorne
Christmas Carol	Dickens

INDEX

148

Nell Peterson

149

FLORA INDEX

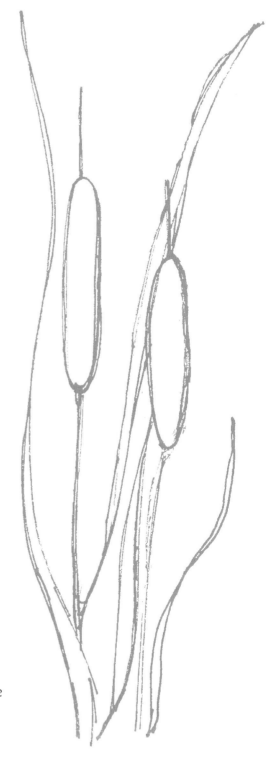

Descendants of Henry Cobb, Elder

1. Henry Cobb, Elder (d. 1679) sp: Sarah Hinckley
   2. Samuel Cobb (b. 1654; d. 1727) sp: Elizabeth Taylor
      3. Jonathan Cobb (b. 1694; d. 1773) sp: Sarah Hopkins (d. 1753)
         4. Jonathan Cobb (b. 1718; d. 1783) sp: Sarah Clark (c. 1702)
            5. Scotto(?) Cobb (b. 1741; d. 1779) sp: Mary Freeman
               6. Elijah Cobb (b. 1768; d. 1848) sp: Mary Pinkham (b. 1770; d. 1835)
                  7. Elijah Cobb (b. 1799; d. 1861) sp: Caroline Snow (b. 1803; d. 1871)
                     8. Helen Cobb (b. 11 Nov 1829-Boston, Suffolk, Mass.; d. 1896)
                        sp: James Atherton Dugan (b. 1827; m. 5 Aug 1852; d. 1860)
                        9. Caroline Atherton Dugan (b. 26 Mar 1853; d. 26 Mar 1941)
                        9. James Winslow Dugan (b. 26 Sep 1854; d. May 1918)
                           sp: Grace E. Kelley (m. 24 Nov 1883)
                        9. Theodore Freeman Dugan (b. 1 Aug 1858; lost at sea)
                        9. Stephen Ives Dugan (b. 31 Aug 1860; d. 3 June 1899)

Chart Courtesy of David Martin, President Cape Cod Genealogical Society

Above: "Copy of Daguerreotype" "Lucy Thacher, Winslow Cobb, Helen Cobb, and Henry Sears"
Helen Cobb is Caro Dugan's mother, born 1829. Winslow is likely Elijah Winslow Cobb, Helen
Cobb's brother who was born in 1827.